Sentences and Paroles

P.J. Murphy taught for nine years in the Simon Fraser University Prison Education Programme. He is the author of two books on Samuel Beckett, *Reconstructing Beckett* and *Critique of Beckett Criticism*, and co-editor with Loyd Johnsen of *Life-25: Interviews With Prisoners Serving Life Sentences.* Jennifer Murphy has done volunteer work in prisons and is completing her Bachelor of Social Work degree at the University College of the Cariboo. P.J. Murphy and Jennifer Murphy live in Kamloops, British Columbia.

SENTENCES AND PAROLES

A Prison Reader

Edited by P. J. Murphy and Jennifer Murphy
With a Foreword by Robert Kroetsch

New Star Books
Vancouver
1998

New Star Books Ltd.
107–3477 Commercial Street
Vancouver, B.C. V5N 4E8

See end of book for full listing of acknowledgments and permissions to reprint.

Design and production by cardigan.com

Cover image: Jeff Wall, *The Old Prison* (1987). Transparency in light box, 70mm × 229cm. Used by permission of the artist.

Printed and bound in Canada by Webcom Ltd.

1 2 3 4 5 02 01 00 99 98

The publisher gratefully acknowledges a grant from the Joanne Brown Endowment, which helped make the publication of *Sentences and Paroles* possible. New Star also wishes to acknowledge the support of the Canada Council, the British Columbia Arts Council, and the Department of Canadian Heritage Book Publishing Industry Development Program.

CANADIAN CATALOGUING IN PUBLICATION DATA
Main entry under title:
Sentences and paroles

ISBN 0-921586-63-9

1. Prisons – British Columbia – Literary collections.
2. Prisoners – British Columbia – Literary collections.
3. British Columbia Penitentiary – Literary collections.
I. Murphy, P. J. (Peter John), 1946– . II. Murphy, Jennifer.

PS8237.P74S46 1998 C810.8'0355 C98-910417-6

PR9194.52.P74S46 1998

He who speaks, he who writes
is above all one who speaks on behalf
of all those who have no voice.

– Victor Serge

Contents

Foreword

Robert Kroetsch

I've abandoned
pretty fairy tales.

Discarded
three minute miracles
Denied
absolution via the mail.

Diana Hartley, writing from Lakeside Correctional Centre, in the opening of her short poem anticipates and celebrates the focus of this anthology. She calls her poem "Untitled," and with the ambiguities of that one word she gives us a clue to the loss of "name" that is involved in entering prison. She begins from that condition and begins to speak, tests her voice, in the careful process of recovering her name by the act of writing.

This anthology takes an unblinking look at writings about life in prison. It looks directly at the question of discourse: how do we write about experience? How, particularly, do we write about the prison experience?

The first question might well be: who gets to speak?

Tradition has kept the prisoner silent, has given voice to those in power. In this anthology, the silent ones transform themselves into poets. They are joined by such distinguished writers as Susan Musgrave and Brian Fawcett. We hear from established writers who have experienced prison life, writers like Andreas Schroeder and Stephen Reid. We hear from working journalists, from the keepers of prisons, from the keepers of prison records. But in the polyphony of voices we hear first of all the breaking of silence.

Diana Hartley in her few lines of poetry invites us, as readers, to abandon our narrative security blankets. We, too, as readers of this anthology, must abandon "pretty fairy tales." We must enter into the labyrinth of experience that is a prison.

We live by narratives, and some of them, some of the time, mislead us. We must be wary of fairy tales, of three minute miracles, of absolution. The narratives of incarceration and punishment do not match up with those inherited and socially approved and socially promulgated stories.

What is the relationship between the words we use in describing an experience and the experience described?

P.J. Murphy and Jennifer Murphy have brought together a selection of writings, accompanied by photographs, that allow us to recognize the connections, the disconnections, the disguises, the naked facts. They begin with "Mute Voices" – a simple and shocking list of the names and numbers and sentences and nationalities of the first prisoners to be transferred to the new B.C. Penitentiary, in 1878. They begin with #1, Ah Tchook, Sentence: 7 years, Nationality: China. They go on to #23, Josephe Flacke, Sentence: 2 years, Nationality: England. And in that catalogue, in that placing of men in a row, we begin to hear the process of silencing – and the process by which muteness might again become voice.

What follows is an abundance. We can only speak against silence by plenitude. We speak against silence not by a single voice but rather by the bewildering force of many voices. This anthology is a full speaking. We hear familiar and famous names: Bill Miner, Sharon Pollock, J. Michael Yates, Claire Culhane. We hear also from an anonymous poet who writes:

A man's voice
cannot be heard
from a numbered
grave.

Where one speaks from, the place of speaking: that too is a question raised by the question of discourse. *Sentences and Paroles: A Prison Reader* is very much an anthology of the voices of men and women who, however confined their place of speaking, are very much alive. They are not granted that life as a gift or as a reward or as a right. In the long tradition of prison writing, they earn for themselves that life by the dangerous act of writing.

Preface

A project such as this needs many helping hands. *Sentences and Paroles* would not have been possible without the support we received over the years from the Simon Fraser University Prison Education Programme's faculty, staff, and students, particularly the editorial collective of *Prison Journal*. Special thanks to Les Merson, Programme Assistant (SFU-PEP), who researched some of the materials used in *Sentences and Paroles* and input an early first draft version of the work. Special thanks also to Debbie Simoneau of the University College of the Cariboo for her patience and care with many versions and revisions of the final typescript. Our thanks also to Professor Jerald Zaslove, Director of SFU's Institute for the Humanities, and his assistant, Trish Graham, for their steadfast support over the years. *Sentences and Paroles* was originally funded by a Canada Council Explorations Grant and subsequently supported by publishing grants from the Institute for the Humanities (SFU) and from President James Wright, University College of the Cariboo. Our thanks are also due to Professor Mason Harris, Department of English, SFU, for his invaluable reader's report.

Valuable research material was supplied by A.E. (Tony) Martin, whose co-operation has been greatly appreciated: Warden Arthur McBride's journals (1878-94); the Penitentiary Service escape file on Bill Miner; a collection of vintage photographs recording the history of the B.C. Penitentiary; and, via the Retired Prison Officers' Association, a complete record of all references to the B.C. Penitentiary in newspapers in B.C. Thanks also to Dr. Glen McDougall of the SFU Prison Education Programme, who located in the SFU archives the disciplinary court record which accompanies the excerpts from Warden McBride's journals.

We would also like to thank the family of the late P.N. Maloff, the Doukhobour historian, who granted permission to quote from his work, *Dukhobortsy, ikh istoriia, zhizn' i bor ba (The Doukhobours: Their History, Life, and Struggle)*.

P. J. Murphy
Jennifer Murphy
Kamloops, B.C., October 1998

Sentences and Paroles

Introduction: Voices from the Pen

I taught in university prison education programmes in British Columbia throughout the 1980s: for three years in the University of Victoria Programme at Matsqui Medium Security in Abbotsford and then for six years at Kent Maximum Security in Agassiz as the Coordinator of the Simon Fraser University Programme. In retrospect, it might appear ironically fitting that after completing a dissertation on Samuel Beckett at the University of Reading I should spend the next decade learning how to read and write gaol; at the time, however, it was simply a disorienting immersion in a strange, new world with its own particular languages and distinct dialects. Teaching at Matsqui in the early 80s was much more a case of ivory bunker than tower. First off was the Matsqui Riot of summer 1981. The institution was heavily damaged in its living unit areas and the Academic Centre was for a period occupied by the inmate population before the inmates were moved out to the sports fields and the infamous Tent City. The university library was left intact, protected by students in the programme, thereby transgressing that venerable prison tradition of torching the last buildings occupied during a riot. The university students led the return from Tent City to the institution proper and played an important role in getting things back to normal (so to speak). We returned to academic time with its semester rituals of various course offerings, time-tables *et al.*, only to be faced in 1983 with Ottawa's cancellation of the university programme. After many months of political manoeuvring, intense lobbying, and strong vocal support from adult education groups across the country, the programme was re-instated.

The riot and the cancellation dramatise the ways in which the university programme was always threatened by various forces within and without the institutions in which it operated. And that very strange hybrid – a university prison education programme – did manage to function, often very successfully, by establishing its own identity as an alternative community in which student and teacher could engage in a critical dialogue with a liberal arts curriculum and its commitment to the humanities.

The University Prison Education Programme had started out as a pilot project at the B.C. Penitentiary in 1972 and, after the Pen's closure in 1980, the programme was established in the new cluster of high-tech prisons throughout the Fraser Valley – Kent, Matsqui, Mountain, as well as at William Head on Vancouver Island (thus giving us more or less comprehensive coverage of the system, since upon sentencing an inmate would typically begin his time at maximum security before proceeding to "cascade" to lower security institutions and then to parole). It was at this point that I entered the prison scene; I left in 1990 to take up another appointment for by that time the writing was clearly on the wall: a series of budget cut-backs and the movement towards a therapeutic model that stressed quick-fix courses in "cognitive skills" marked the beginning of the end. The programme was cancelled in 1993 and this time the cries for its reinstatement fell on deaf ears. So ended a remarkable twenty year venture: an internationally acclaimed prison education programme which had served as the model for similar programmes in the United States and Great Britain was terminated.

Several years (and a couple of books on Beckett) later, I still could not get prison out of my head. The cancellation of the programme supplied the impetus for the completion of *Sentences and Paroles* which I had started working on while teaching in prison. All prison literature is, in a way, a form of testimony, bearing witness to an experience of having been there which is individual yet also part of a collective experience. During the years I taught in prison, I had become increasingly interested in prison literature, that is, writing which employed the carceral image, as well as the writings generated by prisoners themselves, and I developed courses on prison literature which I taught in the prisons and also at the SFU campus in Burnaby. The programme also published *Prison Journal* whose central aims were to provide a forum for the voices of those who are imprisoned and for all those concerned with carrying out a serious examination of the phenomenon of the prison. As an editor of *Prison Journal*, I was necessarily involved with the production of prison writing, collecting various materials, commissioning work on various topics (from in-house as well as outside contributors), and working with prisoner-students on their own writing. With the cancellation of the programme, *Prison Journal* ceased publication and an important organ for voicing the prison world was silenced. There are numerous selections from various issues of *Prison Journal* in

Sentences and Paroles and this is, however indirectly, a testimony to its role in trying to make some sense of the prison experience.

A major character in the story *Sentences and Paroles* plots is the British Columbia Penitentiary, which, of course, no longer exists. After one hundred and two years of solitude, punctuated by periods of intense public scrutiny, the old fortress penitentiary with the postcard view of the Fraser River was declared surplus in 1980, and in 1985 the site was sold to a private developer. The historic gatehouse has been preserved as a coffee shop ("The Pen") and the administrative building is a community centre. Also preserved on the site is an historical marker inscribed as follows:

> ROYAL ENGINEERS BASE OBSERVATORY 1859–60
> At this site the Royal Engineer Detachment determined an absolute value for Longitude of New Westminster, namely 8 hrs., 11 min., 33.3 sec. West Greenwich from a series of lunar observations at Latitude 49 deg., 12 min., 47 sec. North.

The gatehouse and this plaque were two fixed points from which ran the imaginary lines which measured and ordered this province. *Sentences and Paroles* employs a very different type of cartography to locate, to situate in space and time the nature of the prison experience in B.C. Its lines – imaginary and otherwise – aim to encompass a complex reality whose "latitude" and "longitude" can only be traced by the markers of language and its referents. For, although no world is so explicitly bounded by language as a prison – a "sentence" marks the entrance, and "parole" the exit – words in this world do undeniably refer to particular individuals, as well as to the systems or structures which both enclose and encode them. At a time when many of the most influential speculations about language stress various post-modernist approaches in which words are often viewed as counters in a language game that is divorced from historical reality, indeed from the spokesperson, the prison does at least serve as an inescapable reminder of some necessary counter-truths. A purely semiotic analysis of prisons would be literally pointless.

The introductory and concluding sections of *Sentences and Paroles*, "Beginnings" and "Postscripts", supply an enclosing historical framework. Part One, "Sentences", deals with those structures which inscribe the ritual of imprisonment. Inside prison everything that makes up life as it was formerly known is rendered problematical and has to be redefined. The chapters dealing with the key aspects of this redefinition are not, of course, meant to be comprehensive summaries but rather provocative questionings about what that new status entails, via specific comments by particular men and women about their experience. "Arrest", "In a Cell", "The Men", "The Guards", "Working", "Dying", "Surviving", "The Women" and "Voicing" constitute a carceral syntax from which prisoners must try to form their own sentences. Or, at least, rhetorical fragments. One of the most startling and revealing insights for the would-be decipherer of the prison is that this world is, finally – and there is no other word for it – childish. Incarcerated adults are, via bureaucratic and institutional sleight-of-hand, transformed into "children". Then, in the most heavily censored environment in our society, they are asked to act as mature, responsible adults. Amazingly enough, some actually do, as the selections in "Sentences" testify.

Part Two, "Paroles", traces an historical and more individualised progression through a parallel sequence of nine chapters. The selection of photographs on the B.C. Penitentiary by Donald Lawrence blends together images from its past and its present, the past opening a horizon on the present. The chapter on Bill Miner's escape from the B.C. Penitentiary juxtaposes excerpts from the official Penitentiary Service File with poems by Tom Elton from a contemporary prisoner's point of view. The next chapter deals with the Doukhobor situation which, along with the Bill Miner escapade, was one of the most controversial episodes in the first eighty years of the Penitentiary's history. Tom McGauley and Jack McIntosh's commissioned work on the Doukhobors recovered the fascinating story of Vladimir Meier, an expatriate Russian poet who aligned himself with the Sons of Freedom and died under unexplained circumstances at Oakalla. The next three chapters focus on the various "disturbances" which shook the B.C. Pen during the stormy 1970s. The Mary Steinhauser hostage-taking incident is examined from several perspectives: the journalistic accounts followed by reconstructions of the final scene in plays by Christian Bruyere and Sharon Pollock. Thomas Mason Shand's court statement gives a prisoner's view of the problems which plagued the Pen during that decade. The excerpts from Claire Culhane's trilogy of books on prison underscore the need for reform of the "system" from both within and without. John Abbott's interview with Gerry Hannah of the Squamish Five Direct Action Group raises a whole series of new political and social issues of particular relevance to the 80s and 90s. The last two chapters of "Paroles" raise questions concerning the role of education in prison and, more generally, how to make ourselves more literate about the nature and role of the prison itself. "Convocations" juxtaposes valedictorian speeches from the University Programmes at the B.C. Pen and Mountain Institution with Frank Guiney's essay on the teaching of humanities courses developed in the SFU Prison Education Programme at the Carnegie Centre in Vancouver's Eastside. The last chapter focuses on the cancellation of the SFU Prison Education Programme, and the attendant contestation of voices raised over its termination poses important questions about what we hope to gain from our prisons, what they are supposed to be doing.

There is a wealth of materials, indeed an embarrassment of riches, associated with the prison experience in British Columbia. We were fortunate in gaining access to archival materials such as Warden McBride's Journals detailing the first years of the Penitentiary, the Disciplinary Court Record for the same period, the official Penitentiary Service File on Bill Miner's escape, and photographic records of the B.C. Pen from its beginnings to its closure. The inmate publication *Transition* which started publication in the 50s at the B.C. Pen was also a valuable resource in our efforts to trace the development of prison writing in this province. British Columbia has also produced a number of important writers on prison whose work is nationally recognized: for example, Michael Jackson (law professor), Claire Culhane (prison activist), Guy Richmond (prison doctor). Selections from their work and from writers with established reputations who have had some sort of first hand contact with prisons in B.C. give *Sentences and Paroles* an expanded perspective in which a dialogue between outside and inside voices can take place. Susan Musgrave, Brian Fawcett, Andreas Schroeder, Evelyn Lau, J. Michael Yates, Christian Bruyere, Sharon Pollock and Allen Ginsberg – all have in various ways, in a wide range of different types of writing, tried to give expression to their contact with prisons in this province. The works selected and arranged for *Sentences and Paroles* might be regarded as "trans-scriptions", that is, writings which cross over any neat, clear-cut classification of genre boundaries. Poems, stories, plays, essays, official government records and correspondence, reportage, letters to the editor, broadsheets, postcards, interviews, valedictorian addresses, photographs – all are brought to bear on various specific aspects of the prison reality.

While our contemporary literature is full of the metaphors of prison, we tend to forget that the words have specific historical reference and that it is only in our imaginative grasp of both the literal and the literary that a truly creative dialogue can occur. Of course, it is the very absence of such a dialogue that has characterised the history of the modern prison, and this was driven home to me over and over again as I moved back and forth between the inside and outside worlds. From the very beginning, I was, however, also forcibly struck by the liberating paradox that in the prison world there were, in the midst of all the incredible murmuring, bitching, scheming, and maddening nonsense, human voices, vocal presences, persistently – often eloquently – raising fundamental questions about the very ways in which we have organised our society, scripted its rules and values. Prisons are, finally, about freedom and in that residual sense are of vital concern to all of us. If, as Michel Foucault has argued, our institutional structures form a "carceral net", then prison as the most obvious "relay" point in that network can tell us a great deal about ourselves and our convictions. Power, authority, the expropriations of language, the silencing of others, and the struggle to find a voice – these are the essentials in prison, just as they are in the world outside the prison walls. Ioan Davies in *Writers in Prison* has recently underlined that prison writing in Canada is a "backwater": despite our obsession with walls and boundaries our own prison writing has not become part of our "own literary and philosophical sense". *Sentences and Paroles* is one attempt at addressing this situation.

– P.J. Murphy

BEGINNINGS

Prisons are essentially about the exercise of power and a crucial dimension of its authorized control is the determination of who can speak and in what manner. The list of the first inmates at the B.C. Penitentiary we have accordingly entitled "Mute Voices". Excerpts from Warden McBride's Journal afford only skeletal outlines of these itemized inmates as human presences. Note, for example, the case of Convict O'Connor who was denied permission to write to the U.S. consul until "his conduct was better". Horse Billy's sore foot gets more attention than many of the prisoners' requests. The prison as a virtually self-contained domestic economy is the dominant impression gained from the reams of mundane details in the Warden's Journals. The June 13th 1886 entry – "Vancouver Burnt down today" – is only an afterthought, a piece of marginalia. The Disciplinary Court Records speak for themselves: many of the punishments meted out are, in fact, for violation of the "silent system" which was in force – even talking to oneself in ones's own cell could lead to an inscription of punishment in the Court Record. The "Fly Sheet" is, arguably, the first authentic piece of prison literature in B.C. Its accusations of abuse at the B.C. Penitentiary led to an official inquiry when Senator Thomas Robert McInnis, uncle of the penitentiary's steward, made a statement in the Senate supporting the charges. Inspector J.G. Moylan's report completely exonerated the officers, praised the way the prison was operated and firmly closed the book on further inquiries. Throughout the history of the B.C. Pen, remarkably similar situations would, however, occur again and again.

Mute Voices

Adapted from Warden Arthur McBride's B.C. Penitentiary Journals, 1878–1889

Name	*Official Number*	*Sentence*	*Nationality*
Ah Tchook	1	7 years	China
John Brown	2	10 years	Portugal
Leo	3	14 years	B.C.
John Steele	4	15 years	Ireland
John Hart	5	5 years	England
Peter Adair	6	14 years	Scotland
Baptiste Tomas	7	6 years	U.S.A.
James Brown	8	10 years	Canada
Charlie Brading	9	4 years	Holland
Antony Simmons	10	7 years	West Indies
Frederick Harrison	11	5 years	England
Jim	12	2 years	B.C.
Louie	13	2 years	B.C.
Ah Kew	14	3 years	China
Ah Nee	15	3 years	China
Ah Took	16	2 years	China
John Dawdry	17	5 years	England
John Elliott	18	3 years	B.C.
John Jordan	19	15 years	Ireland
Edward Morgan	20	3 years	U.S.A.
James Kelly	21	3 years	Ireland
Augustus Dieusey	22	2 years	France
Josephe Flacke	23	2 years	England

The above listed convicts were the first admitted to the B.C. Penitentiary on the 28th and 29th September, 1878. It is noted that the majority of sentences were handed down by Sir Matthew Begbie, the famous hanging judge.

Leo #3 died in September 1879.

Peter Adair #6 was pardoned October 1882.

James Brown #8 escaped May 1881.

The above mentioned convicts were received from Provincial Gaols in Victoria and New Westminster.

Other Voices

Excerpts from BC Penitentiary Warden Arthur McBride's Journals, 1878–1889

Mr. Falding arrived in New Westminster with a message from Mr. Moylan, Inspector of Penitentiaries, instructing me to go to Victoria and bring two of my Guards to remove the convicts from Victoria Gaol to Penitentiary New Westminster.

September 25th, 1878: I went to Victoria as instructed.

September 26th: I received eight Snider Rifles complete with seven hundred and eighty rounds of Ball Cartridge from the Military Storekeeper Victoria.

September 27th: Received from the Sheriff of Victoria Twelve Convicts and brought them safely to the Penitentiary arriving about 5 P.M. Supper was already provided for them as ordered.

September 28th: Received from the Sheriff of New Westminster Eleven Convicts, which I conveyed safely to Penitentiary. Some were heavily ironed and I procured a Stage to bring them out.

September 29th: Visited the Convicts at their Breakfast, Dinner and Supper, and afterwards went to the wing.

September 30th: According to orders I received from Mr. Moylan, I had single Irons made with Chain attached and substituted for the heavy Irons.

October 1st to 5th: Nothing unusual occurred. Visited the Convicts as usual at their meals and in the wing, on the 5th Received Convict Timothy O'Callagher.

October 6th to 10th: Nothing unusual occurred. Visited the convicts as usual at their Meals and in the wing. Received on the 10th Convict Peter Antigo. On the 7th Captain Robinson received the Contract to supply Penitentiary with one hundred and twenty Ton of Coal.

November 1st, 1883: . . . I have taken the shackles off the Convicts, each of them was brought into my office and they all promised to conduct themselves well for the future. I had all the guards in the Office previous to taking the irons off and informed them what I was going to do and cautioned them to be very careful. Was present at dinner and visited the wing at 4 P.M. & 7 & 9 P.M.

November 2nd: . . . Was present at dinner & Read the rules to the Convicts, discharged Convicts Ah Jake & Young Dock Siil. . . .

April 17th, 1884: Visited the wing at 8 a.m. & went over all of the building and was present at dinner. At about 4:30 P.M. Convict Barry made an attempt to Murder Guard Fitzgerald by Stabbing him with a Fork in the face and afterwards twice in the Arm. He was brought down and placed in irons, will be brought before the Supreme Court at next Assizes. I have confined him in his Cell on half rations until that time, the 7th of May, next. Convicts Bell & Johnston went to the assistance of Guard Fitzgerald, will report their Conduct to Inspector.

May 3rd: . . . Guard Stevens came on duty under the influence of Liquor. I dismissed him.

May 7th: Visited the wing at 7:30 a.m. Went all over the building. Went to town to attend the Assizes. Barry the Convict was sentenced to Ten Years additional Imprisonment in Penitentiary to run concurrent from this date with former sentence. Visited the wing at 10 P.M.

July 22nd: . . . Convict O'Connor came into my office today and asked leave to write to the U.S. Consul. I informed him that I would let him write when his conduct was better, but not until then, as it was a privilege granted for good conduct. . . .

July 26th: . . . Guard Quilty and the Steward went as usual to Con Barry's Cell to have him Shaved, in coming out he threw a handful of lime in Guard Quilty's face and then took hold of him, the Steward Struck Barry with the Cell Key and put him Back in his Cell, afterwards Barry was searched and a Knife found on him made from the Iron hoop of his bucket. . . .

July 28th: . . . Convict Barry had the wooden door of his Cell closed and would not open it, or Pass his bucket out. I sent for the Doctor and Had the evidence of Guard Quilty and the Steward taken down in oath. I then awarded 60 lashes with cats to Barry which was given to him in the presence of the Surgeon . . .

July 30th: . . . Had the door of Convict Barry's Cell put in repair by Mr. Blackie and a Cross Bar put on.

October 16th: . . . At 1 P.M. Convict, No. 118, Thomas O'Connor having been reported was brought into my office. I ordered him to have Irons put on him until his conduct would permit of their being removed. He then asked me if he could write to the Judge, I told him not until his conduct would be better. He then made a turn & jumped through my office window, opened the window and Guard Hutchinson and Trade Instructor McKenzie jumped out and pursued him. Guard Smyth also followed him. O'Connor got hold of a ladder that had been used repairing a Stand and after Guard Called upon to stop & when He was on top of the fence McKenzie Fired his revolver at him and the Bullet struck him a little below the Knee. He was then brought Back and the Dr. sent for. Visited the wing at 5 P.M. . . .

November 1st: . . . John Budge came on duty as night Guard in Place of Guard Lehar who resigned. . . .

November 4th: Guard Smyth informed me at 7:10 am that Guard Rodgers had Shot and Killed Guard Sterry in their house at Sappertown, I ordered him to take a Horse and go to town & see that Rodgers was taken into Custody and also to inform Coroner Trew. When He came back which was immediately He informed me that Rodgers had surrendered himself.

Coroner Trew held an Inquest and Verdict was that Guard Sterry came to his death by being shot with a Pistol Ball in the hands of Guard Rodgers. Visited the wing at 5 P.M. & 9:30 P.M.

November 5th: . . . Guard Budge Resigned today and Mr. Downey took his place as night Guard. H.W. Ottan and G. Tirhiem came on duty this day as Guards in Place of the late Guard Sterry & Rodgers.

July 25th, 1885: . . . Horse (Billy) while carting oats got a nail forced into his hind foot about one Inch. He is quite lame.

July 28th: . . . Sent for Mr. John Reid (Farrier) to See Horse (Billy). He lanced and dressed the sore foot. . . . read the rules to the Guards. . . .

August 1st: . . . Edward W. King came on duty as Night Guard in the place of A. Gordon (Resigned).

August 3rd: Mr. Reid came to see Horse today.

August 5th:... Convict Murphy complained that his meat and soup was bad. Dr. Trew examined it and pronounced it good....

August 10th:... Mr. J. Reid came to see the (Horse) Billy's foot today.

August 15th: ... Mr. Walter Blackie came to examine the Sick Horse's foot.

August 23rd:... Mr. Blackie came to see Horse Billy.

January 26th, 1886:... I asked Dr. Trew today if it was right in his opinion to keep shackles on Convict O'Connor while he was complaining of his leg (in day time). The Dr. said that he believed that O'Connor was humbugging and that in his opinion it was right to keep the shackles on him. Convict No. 127 J. Kelly was allowed to have an undershirt, when the steward gave him one, he would not wear it, as it had been worn before by some other Convict. Dr. Trew ordered it and said that the Shirt would do for Kelly.

June 13th:... Visited the wing at 8:15 A.M. and at 8:30 A.M.. Saw Convicts to Church and visited the wing at 12:30 P.M. – Vancouver Burnt down today.

The 'Fly Sheet'

"A fly sheet printed in Washington territory containing the vilest slanders and most barefaced falsehoods against the administration of this Penitentiary [the B.C. Penitentiary] and some of its most deserving Officers was put in circulation in Victoria about twelve months ago. The production was the work of two of the most depraved and hardened criminals that ever cursed, with their presence, any penitentiary in the Dominion. It was one of them who, coming across from Seattle, distributed in a few hours, the untruthful and libelous publication and made his escape to American territory before his arrest could be effected."

– John S.D. Thompson, Minister
Report of the Minister of Justice for the Year Ending 30th June 1889

The "fly sheet" Thompson refers to was a cheaply printed pamphlet that accused the officers of treating inmates unfairly and inhumanely, of administering corporal punishment for trivial offences, of neglecting the sick and showing favouritism. All efforts to locate this "fly sheet" drew a blank. As Heather J. MacMillan, Archivist, State, Military and Cultural Records Section, Ottawa, stated: "In all probability, the 'fly sheet' was printed on very thin paper that may not have survived the years, or perhaps it was never actually filed with government records."

Disciplinary Court Record

British Columbia Penitentiary Excerpts from 1878–1881

Date	*Name*	*Report*	*Reporting Officer*	*Punishment other than loss of remission time*	*Days remission forfeited carried to ledger*
1878					
Dec. 31	John Steele	Attempting suicide	J. Wiggins	Reported insane, see Dr. certificate	8 days
1879					
Jan. 21	Ah Tow	Insubordinate conduct and disrespect	Bullen	Admonished.	
Jan. 21 & 22	Augustus Dieusey	Pilfering meat & mustard from kitchen	Bullen	Admonished.	
Jan. 29 & 30	Peter Antigo	Insubordination while at work	H. Kehoe	Deprived of supper for one night and loss of tobacco for one week	
Feb. 27th	Jacob	Ran away from his gang. Was called to stop but ran on until caught by Guard Wiggins and brought back.	H. Kehoe	Ordered thirty lashes with cats, and confined to solitary cel. until further orders, with chains and bread & water diet for four meals.	Remained the night in solitary.
March 31	Peter Antigo	Idling his time at his work and being insolent when spoken to by the guard.	B.P. Graham	Deprived of lamp in his cell for one month and bread and water diet for one meal.	
May 4th	John Tawdry	Talking in his cell	B.P. Graham	Admonished.	
May 4th	Peter Antigo	Talking in his cell	B.P. Graham	Admonished.	
May 31st	Peter Antigo	Refusing to work	J. Morey	Hard bed for three nights and deprived of lamp in his cell for three nights	
July 3rd	Ah Tow	Cutting his drawers	Bullen	Loss of remission for five days.	5
July 4th	John Elliott	Insolence at the breakfast table saying that he would rather be punished than starved to death	Bullen	24 hours in dark cell with bread and water diet.	

1880

Feb. 26	John Indian	For refusing to work	J. Davey	48 hours in dark cell on bread and water diet and deprived of lamp in his cell until he goes to work.	
March 5	James Pertin	For assault on Convict Laplante	J. Davey	Ordered to wear a chain	
March 9	George Alep	Talking while at work & idling his time	J. Fitzgerald	Loss of remission ten days	10
March 9	James Walsh	Talking while at work & idling his time	J. Fitzgerald	Loss of remission ten days.	10
March 9	George Robinson	Talking while at work & idling his time	J. Fitzgerald	Loss of remission ten days.	10
March 29	Peter Antigo	For talking in their cells	J. Fitzgerald	Admonished.	
March 29	George Alep	For talking in their cells	J. Fitzgerald	24 hours dark cell on bread & water diet.	
April 9th	Peter Antigo	Talking whilst at work	H. Kehow	deprived of tobacco and lamp for one month.	
April 9th	George Alep	Talking whilst at work	H. Kehow	deprived of tobacco and lamp for one month.	
April 9th	Isaac Vertin	Talking whilst at work	H. Kehow	deprived of tobacco and lamp for one month.	

1881

Nov. 9th	John Morrison	For using threatening language and calling the Dep. Warden a cannibal	J. Fitzgerald	To be confined to a separate cell with such diet as the surgeon shall pronounce fit & sufficient & also no bedding until further orders. Released 15th Nov.
Dec. 10th	John Morrison	Breach of prison rules by constantly complaining & finding fault with his rations, also speaking to the surgeon without permission.		Admonished
Dec. 29th	John Morrison	Disobedience of orders & insolent language to the Deputy Warden	J. Fitzgerald	Bread and water for nine consecutive meals with solitary confinement & with blankets and afterwards to remain in solitary cell until he promises to conduct himself. *Under surgeon's care, released Jan. 14/82*

PART 1

SENTENCES

1

ARREST

Arrest initiates the ritual of incarceration, sentencing to follow. These four selections, in very different ways, underscore key aspects of this first stage. Frank Guiney and John Abbott's poems deal with the judicial process in its personal and public applications. Stephen Reid's ballad "On the Road, Again" describes the transportation to a prison: on "public display", "Eleven new convicts riding / a century to the wall". George L. Taylor's disquieting short story "Frame a Day" fabricates an arrest brought about by the maddening logic of a dreadful series of puns. All the sections converge, in one way or another, on the question of noise versus voice, rhetoric versus poetry, reason versus madness – all terms to be defined by which side of the prison fence you are on. They all testify to a fundamental shift in identity; as Victor Serge summed up in discussing his own arrest in *Men in Prison:* "I had crossed the invisible boundary. I was no longer a man, but a man in prison. An inmate."

Fall Assizes

Frank Guiney · 1981

Two guys
arguing
about the radio
the guy
who blasted
his wife's liver out
last week
because
he suddenly realized
she owned
half his life

wants quiet

and the kid
who put six inches
of cold hunting knife
into a warm chest
for
thirty-five dollars
a chargex card
and the loan of a car
says fuck you
turn it up

he needs noise
to hear the music

his young ears
are accustomed to it
the widower
rips the wires off the wall

rips the speaker off the wall
the kid screams
like it was him
ripped off the wall

next morning
only one murderer
appeared in court

according to the radio

which was
right back up there
on the wall

like
always

The Rossland Courthouse

John Abbott · 1982

In Cathedral lights, Chartres blue
three boars' heads emblazoned withal
Matthew Baillie Begbie
who'd hang
as often as he'd ride

white wigs dead in the sunshine
dust driven in buffets of air
as formula speeches
drag themselves
from pew to pulpit and back.

The accused
is the one the shotgun points out
click, shak, jack a round
"unit 1 unidentified male subject approaching
south west corner . . .
tan Plymouth moving east, Alberta
licence plates watch the . . ."

the radio belt barks
to the guards
who watch the doors,
the windows,
slam the doors
as they guard the courthouse

the man on the dais
jumps in his eyes
the accused sits in a clear field
of fire.

On the Road, Again

Stephen Reid · 1985

Staring out the wirescreen windows
of a dirty grey bus
wearing stainless-steel leg-irons
on a chain for the coast.

Eleven new convicts riding
a century to the wall.
Verdicts still ringing, numbers
slashed freshly across the chest.
Three days and four nights on a
cross-country roll, in blue denim
coveralls wearing a century and a half
of time.

Overweight guards with underarm stains,
sit inside caged personalities.
A finger in their nose, a 12-gauge in their lap,
they're working on yesterday's answers.

This morning we pulled over in
Portage La Prairie, stumbled out on
public display in a service station parking lot.
Some motorists tried to sneer, others turned away,
but their daughters waved to us anyway.
On board, first-timers replied with
insolence; the ones who still cared looked
down. My eyes just stayed on the 12-gauge shotguns.
I already knew the 99 names of hell.

Pavement roaring down my throat,
destination on my mind. I've got a
three-time hole in my heart and I'm
all out of questions this time.

Turn signal's clicking; I've got a
lockpick in my brain.
Come the next stop, I'll try to
break this goddamned chain.

Frame a Day

George L. Taylor · 1987

It all occurred on that particular morning, it was quite early as a matter of fact. From my bed i watched the sunbeam almost motionlessly broaden beneath my windowsill, my senses sleepily partial to this phenomenon. And then my ears became partial to the dog continuously making an ill noise outside the window where Mr. Sunbeam invited himself into my bedroom.

Slowly climbing out of bed, i donned my robe and walked outdoors around to the side of my house and found the mongrel, a dozy look on its face, barking at its imagination. Instantly i yelled "Shut up!" but the dog wasn't listening, so i repeated louder this time, "SHUT UP!!" but that didn't do much, so i yelled louder than before, "SHUT THE HELL UP!!!!" but the dog was short of mentality and didn't take heed to my warning, so reaching down to the side of my house, my hand gripped a scrap piece of two by four, which i brought to the dog's head.

Then the mongrel listened, it was very quiet.

Trudging back to my humble abode, i flopped back into bed and ditto dreamland, but my doorbell Rang and RAng and RANg and RANG bringing me to rise from the tranquility of rest. Peering out my front window through the crack in the drapes, my eyes focused on an ugly fat-faced bitch with an evil look in her eyes.

Swinging open my front door, almost instantly my ears caught a flood of threats, insults and foul language. I didn't like it so i slammed the door in her face. Walking down the hallway to my semi-lit bedroom, the increasing tempo of doorbell ringing halted me in my tracks.

Swinging around, my pace quickened towards the door. Annoyed i opened it and mixed the four letter word with another and slammed the door in her face a bit harder this time, but the annoyance started to ruin the expensive finish on my oak panel door by kicking it quite violently.

The gun felt nice and balanced in my right hand. Swinging the door wide open on its creaky hinges, my gun and i both gave her a piece of our minds. She was very good about it after that. She went to sleep right on the doorstep.

Yawning, i headed down my hallway back to misty dreamland. I had only acquired a minor amount of winks, when i was awakened by an anticipating knock at my front door. "The Bitch Must Have Insomnia," i thought.

Opening the door i was met by a whole bunch of men in code, some lying on the front lawn relaxing, some skulking behind my hedges and quite a few sunday driving down the street, and there was two of them in front of me with sunglasses and really nice guns in their hands and i was honoured they came to visit me.

"Can i get you a coffee?" i cheerfully inquired. They both exchanged puzzled glances. Tying my hands behind me with chrome, they took me for a joyride through town to their clubhouse, but they didn't look happy and then i realized something was wrong and i was in deep trouble. "BELIEVE ME MEN IN CODE, I DIDN'T MEAN TO SHOUT AT THE LADY," and from that moment on i believed i had been FRAMED.

2

IN A CELL

"The present minute is infinite. But time does not exist. A madman's logic? Perhaps. I know how much profound truth there is in it. I also know that a captive is, from the very first hour, a mentally unbalanced person." The works in this section discuss various ways of establishing a new equilibrium attuned to the rhythms of time and space in the prison. Bruce Chester's "Spook" is a comic version of the above lines from Victor Serge: dungeons may be "conducive to insanity", but "I'm all here." Jack McCann details the terrible deprivations of solitary confinement in SCU (Special Correction Unit) at the B.C. Pen, also known as "the hole", "the Penthouse", or "the Fraserview Hilton". One way in which McCann survived was to write poems. The prison writings of the gypsy Peter Farrell, while technically semi-literate, have a startling poetic power. In my interview with him in *Prison Journal* 7 (1988), Farrell commented on the role of his writing in prison: "It's just a way to keep my mind off the penny shit that goes on in here. But when I do write, some of it is true but I don't say which is true because if I was to do that, I'd get stinged from my family . . . So I'd rather write something positive, yet negative, and it all works out in the end for somebody in here." The poems by Andreas Schroeder and Jeff Ewert talk about the disturbing self-reflexivity that goes with life in a cell and which, at privileged moments, may even be self-illuminating.

Spook

Bruce Chester · 1984

Being in a dungeon is said to be
conducive to insanity
by liberal sages.

"How very wrong" I hum
my toe nails clicking like
out of tune castanets
upon the damp concrete floor
"I'm all here"

Prisoner of Isolation

Michael Jackson · 1983

At the time of the trial [1975] Jack McCann had probably spent more time in solitary than any other prisoner in the Canadian penitentiary system. This is how he described his feelings about his years in solitary confinement.

I think treatment in SCU is terrible. I am reminded every day I wake up and when I go to sleep. Men put up there with no concrete reason, no way of knowing how long they'll be up there, no decent answers to questions. No good communication to classification officers – the lies, the deceit, the stringing along, no one would ever be straight with me. The harm it had on others was most affecting on me. It hurt me, I was close to that point myself many times. I had no physical outlet for emotions. I used to break down and cry. Persons mutilating would not even get stitched up by a doctor, just bandaged by nurses and then brought back. I've never slashed up, maybe I am a moral coward, but I want to die my way, not their way. . . .

All you live on in SCU is bitterness and hatred. For some guys that's not enough. Their hatred reaches the point when they have to see blood, even if it is their own. . . .

Up there I have fears of losing my sanity, fears of losing my friends, fears of myself. There is no physical fear, I can put up with that.

Jack McCann gave evidence that in 1967, while he was in SCU, on three successive days other prisoners slashed themselves. He was given the job of cleaning up the blood in their cells. McCann "begged and pleaded to be let out of solitary." Yet another prisoner slashed himself. McCann could take no more and he set himself on fire in his cell. He described to the court what he saw as the flames engulfed him: "I remember watching the space beneath the door get bigger. I thought I could crawl beneath it and be free . . . I wanted to get out – I don't care if I die, I never want to go back to that position again." In a letter to a friend written in July 1972, McCann explained his feelings:

What am I anyway? a moral coward because I can't end . . . Do they really think I'm a mental case that can't associate with other people. If this is their thinking, why keep me here when they can send me to the bughouse. I'll tell you why, because they don't know what I am and they reject the words of the people who know me. You know something, I don't think they believe I'm human. They can't! To them I'm some sort of object, yet undefined, that they must fool around with once in a while to amuse themselves. Dear, I'm not only frustrated, I'm bitter. I think I'm a real first-class cynic. I question their motives on anything or everything and don't believe a word they say any more. I am . . . envious. Not envious of your freedom on the street as much as your freedom to the right to fresh air and freedom to the sunshine.

McCann gave evidence that when he was returned to the population after five years of solitary confinement he felt "lost in the fresh air." When McCann escaped in 1973, he got in touch with a member of the press and asked him to publicize the condition of men in solitary confinement. He also stated that his escape was precipitated by rumours that he was going back into solitary.

Dr. Stephen Fox, in commenting on the effects of solitary on McCann, said, "self-immolation, setting yourself on fire . . . is as far into it as I can imagine anyone can go, into total insanity, of reduction to nothing, the hopelessness, the meaninglessness, the violence, the cycle of destruction." On the cumulative effect of McCann's long years in solitary, Dr. Fox states that "there is a scepticism and a doubt about the nature of himself and his own abilty to deal in any positive way with another human being. There is a serious undermining of the capacity to feel and to communicate. There is a substantial anger which endangers everyone, endangers himself and those around him, not physically, but endangers his relationship to them."

Jack McCann wrote a series of poems while in solitary. One of these, entitled "My Home is Hell," was read to the court. Here are some of the stanzas:

My home is hell in one small cell
That no man wants to own,

For here I spend my life condemned
A man the world disowns.

So I, the damned, within walls crammed
Lie in my man-made grave
A man all men condemned for sin
But no man strives to save.

Each lonely dawn that night spawns
I stand and face the wall
In bitterness and loneliness
I await the whistle's call.

Men scream and yell within my hell
But I'm a man alone,
My tears of pain, like bitter rain,
Spill down on naked stone.

Here every gate is one of hate,
Love has no place to hide
For each lost fool who breaks a rule
The way to hell is wide.

The things men hate and mutilate,
Are those that all men value.
The mind of man, the will within,
The spirit that God gives you.

The right to sin, but rise again,
A free man, not a slave,
To find a friend and at the end,
Escape a pauper's grave.

I cannot tell to those in hell,
The dreams I send above.
Now how the shrill of whistles kill,
Each passing thought of love.

Within these walls that never fall,
The damned all come to know,
The row of cells – the special hell,
Called Solitary Row.

Where seconds cheat and hunger eats
The belly of each slave,
Where gas is shot and each man rots
In his lonely grave.

To sleepless nights, to glaring lights,
To guns and bars and chains,
To walls of stone and men alone,
In years I can't regain.

To those who take my dreams and make
Me live in hell forever,
To those who lash – and try to smash,
The human spirit forever.

To those who steal the things I feel
And sow my heart with sorrow,
Each farewell I bid in hell,
Is lost in each tomorrow.

What you are about to hear is True and Faults

Peter Farrell · 1988

Sunday September 20th, 1987

H Block, Kent Institution

It begain in the New Westminster holding cells for court, it was a 8×10 cell, that held one 60 year old man. He was lyining on a platick couch using a roll of toilet paper as a pillow telling me of his lifes tragites and why he was in lock up. He said that he was at home ready to take his life with a butcher knife he had take but end of the knife and place it against the wall and was going to run into it with his body. But just then two Rouckie cops intered from the front door of his house, saying put down the knife. The old man replyed come and take it from me. The two cops pulled out their guns and said again put down the knife before you hurt yourself. The old man said go ahead and shutt sevear times saying that he wouldn't put down the knife, can't you see that I am trying to take my life, leaning forward and backwards. Just then they had desideed to fire on him twise in the stumet and once in the lower stumet that shot through the lift cheek of his ass. The old man was momble something as he drop to the floor, you duty basters you shot me.

Three days later wacking up in a hospital bed piss off at the world closing his eyes and their he dide.

looking out a window

Peter Farrell · 1988

looking out the window of my apt i could see in to the Country Jug and i was watching the inmate in his cell putting pictures on the walls and getting frusated with doing time.

day after day i would go to the window to see if it might be different for the person who sit in confinmat

but i had other thing's do do then look out of window's.

"yes i had all the reasons to be looking out windows but not to watch people doing time. my thing was to take care of a little matter for Mr. Nelson at the courthouse that day and that is why i had been looking out my apt window for day's on end, but the time came for me to do my job for the head crime boss of Beverly Hills "Mr. Nelson".

As the story was told to me, this guy "Nick Cairo" was going to tell the cops all about "Mr. Nelson's business in the under world and "i was to see that" that didn't happen.

and now come the time for me to get this rat out of the picture and i did by leting him have it right out side at the court house three times in the head and i started to run down the street to get my car but i know that i would never make it"

the cops wear all over me and letting bullits go like crazy and "now in here in hell doing the time of my life and i mean the rest of my life.

Four-Right-Sixteen

Andreas Schroeder · 1987

Sometimes I chant to myself
where I have been

It loosens briefly
I move too slowly
It hardens again

How desperate must a man
become
to finally say what curls and twists
inside him

Three years clutching the same burned-out
woman,
and I didn't even know
until later
that emptiness is catching

Now two years of prison
of staying alive only
by standing as close as possible
to the crazy ones
who make one feel, at least now and then,
that there are no mysteries

I've tired of using my friends
to keep myself breathing,
No doubt they're tired too,
Puzzled anger like stones
falling just short of my back
as I walk away . . .

Every night I sit in the middle
of my bed
trying to row myself
to sleep

I want to
I want to
I want to
I want

so many sudden departures

These nights when I lie
carefully breathing in the dark
I can hear
throughout my entire body

The slow purposeful ticking
of something insidiously
biding its
time.

The Man in the Mirror

Jeff Ewert · 1989

The man in the mirror
is a friend of mine.
I can reach him most of the time
but so often he talks to me
while checking his reflection.
I wish he wasn't so worried about how he is perceived.
No one here is half as concerned about his appearance
as he appears to be.
Stiff-necked, so as to not upset his freshly combed hair,
he moves away from
the mirror on the wall. He seats himself and to my
surprise
he reaches out
and picks up a hand-held mirror strategically placed
within arm's reach of his desk,
and he checks his hair to make sure he didn't
upset it along the way of
his six-and-a-half-foot journey from the sink to his desk.
I wish I could help him but I don't know what I could say and
even if I did I
wouldn't know whether to say it to him or to the mirror
because I am starting
to wonder which is really him, the reflection or the
three-dimensional version
I see.

In a desperate attempt to help him I reach out
and grab the mirror to talk
to him and I see he's not there. Instead, I see
my own reflection staring back
at me and I realize that before I can ever consider
telling him about his problems,
I should first look at myself and my own problems.

The two men in the mirrors are friends of mine.

3

THE MEN

Victor Serge likens the prison to a mill which grinds men up. In *Men in Prison*, he portrays the "real men" who are able to resist this process: "The outlaw has no illusions about society's values and knows neither faith nor law; but has self-respect, the knowledge of his own strength, and the respect of other 'men' – the strong. 'I'm a man!': All his pride is summed up in these words." These values are still part of the prisoner's code today. John Rives' "Wouldn't it be Fun to be a Badman" is in some ways an ironic treatment of the romantic myth of the outlaw that is so entrenched in our popular stereotypes. Brian Fawcett's poems dedicated to prisoners he got to know while teaching creative writing at Matsqui Institution present two very different sides to the question of masculinity – the machismo of "The Gun" and the life rhythms of "Make the Body Move". The excerpts from Andreas Schroeder's prison memoir *Shaking It Rough* present a striking series of images depicting the "common nervous system" to which all the prisoners are "hooked up", like members of a "primitive tribe". "Of the Fittest", an anonymous work by a member of Kent Institution's General Population, talks of the deadly conformity which the "inmate code" imposes upon its members. In most Canadian prisons, the population is divided into two distinct groupings, General Population (GP) and Protective Custody (PC), thus rendering problematic the very definition of "men in prison".

Wouldn't It Be Fun To Be a Badman?

John Rives · 1988

What if people feared me?

In High School,
how I'd fantasize.
Though now I feel as dirty
and untouchable, as leprous
as some people say I am.

But, I've changed
I tell you!
Good to bad to worse to
not so good to better –
than – before to to to

I feel the same,
I watch the dumb
programs on TV.
And after all that's
happened, how
I flagellate myself
for tuning in

and seeing things in colour,
as before.

Perhaps I live
off your fear –
it is appalling.

And it hurts when old
friends shy away.

The Gun · TO RICK WILSON

Brian Fawcett · 1988

Somewhere in that big world you dream about,
in the black and white of we versus them
a man loads the gun, adjusts earplugs,
and prepares to practise death.

He squeezes the trigger,
and across a gravel shooting range
bullets shred their paper human targets

But in his black and white it's not a shooting range at all.
He's in a busy street that suddenly is filled with Enemies –
Commie Pervert Sexfiend Coloured Objects up to no Good Business.

As they stare at his gun
he sees delicious terror blooming in their eyes,
made more alive by sheer mayhem,
their choked cries anthem to his private government
the men and women and small children dropping democratically
as he fires into the reality
he creates with the gun.
Then, in a burst of spontaneity
he runs patterns of pug marks
across the walls of a buildingthupthupthupthupthup
as the blood puddles,
then runs into the gutters like a torrent
of Evil Expunged.

And you tell me
What the hell,
why fight that urge?
Why not give in to those moments
of perfect belligerence?

Yeah, sure.
Why not beat up on our wives and kids
if the urge is there, why not
pick up that lead pipe over there,
why not put a hit on that perfect stranger in an alley?

In this kind of world
it's better to kick shit
than to eat it, you say,
sure that the homily covers every complexity.

Just a minute, I say. Nothing is that simple.
Do you know what happens
when we get our rocks off from TV violence,
where the staccato of the machine pistol
or the snap of a fist breaking a face
is tricked out into a song-and-dance routine
right out of Disneyland?

That's only fun, you say,
nobody real gets hurt.

I repeat again. Nothing is that simple.
These days, I say, people can't tell the difference
between Art and Life
don't know how and where
each turns into lies or the beginning of absolute violence:
it may just be a slicko in a leisure suit
trying to sell us some product we don't want or need,
or it may end up with people bleeding in the street.

Maybe there was a time when the directors directed,
the producers produced
and the writers wrote.
Those certainties aren't there for us.
The set-pieces no longer stay set and predictable

and nothing chills our souls on cue
or allows us to go to our beds at night safe.

And so you shrug and say
Yeah, it's all anger now
and you want the gun for yourself.

But you don't have the gun, it's only
a picture of a gun in a magazine
you bring to frighten me
and I'm glad there's no gun here
because you're off with that man
and I don't trust either of you.

If you were out in the world
you could shake up that man,
or fuck him
(or outsmart him with your big cool brain
if you're really smart).

But you're here in this prison
because you're not very smart
and he's probably sitting outside the wire
in his windowed tower
reading that same magazine.

And he's got the gun.

Make the Body Move · TO BOB ANDREWS

Brian Fawcett · 1988

For hours we argue as equals
asking what freedom of the body is
and what collective life and love and loyalty
can ask of it.

Then, abruptly, comes the knocking on the door,
buzzers bray across the razor-wire enclosures,
the guards inform me it is time to leave
so they can count the men who'll stay the night,
who've made mistakes, are innocent-and other euphemisms.

The men the guards believe belong to them.

I pack up my heavy teacher's books,
pass through the many-gated inner world of men controlling men,
pass through the final lighted steel mesh fence
into the wind and rain and dark.

You go back to your cell
to let the rhythm of the count resume.

All the way out I hear you last words:
"Make the body move," you said.
"Feel what it is to be free."
I walk across the parking lot
and feel no freedom,
no movement but my own,
singular and forced by cold and wet and wind.

Then I get into my car and drive home
into the swirling responsibilities
I call my life, counting them as I drive.

But later, walking home from the store
with a quart of milk under my arm
the rain starts again.

And with its rhythm the ground
begins to move beneath me,
neither chaos nor a count of prisoners
but a soft dance of numberless single things:
the glistening streets, the rain,
the buying and carrying of milk, each
the movement of a body greater than my own.

Sure this collusion is obscure.
And sure, my unnumeric revelation is absurd.
Such freedom (you will say) is nothing
but a cruel hallucination
set up by desire and privilege
like any civilized and civilizing ecstasy.
How can one man be free
While others take the count behind barred doors and metal fences?

I see no wire mesh here,
no bars or razor wire
to block my casual transit through the streets,
and for a moment the body I am in
is sweet and wet, a home.

I walk back aimlessly,
content with shiny cars, tattered hedges,
the glow of television
in the living rooms of every house.
Each step I take a dance of neutral liberty:

I move,
the ignorant body moves,
and that is what there is

Fragments 11 and 19 from *Shaking It Rough*

Andreas Schroeder · 1976

11.

It seemed, at first, while I was watching mostly myself and not others, that my good days and bad days had their source demonstrably inside me. When I felt depressed (or not), I could always find in myself a perfectly good reason for these feelings.

But in time I began to notice that when I mentioned my moods to others, they almost always felt the same way, and when I felt miserable, the pall apparently hovering over the entire cell block wasn't simply a projection of my own depression. After I'd grown more accustomed to being Inside and had gotten to know a much larger number of inmates, I found that to an astonishing extent the prison poulation's feelings moved and changed in unison; a bad day for one tended to be a bad day for all. And this did not appear to be the result of any one inmate taking his cue from another. Something of which all inmates had become a part, some common nervous system into which we had all become plugged, appeared to affect us all more or less at the same time. We had, in some way, effectively become a primitive tribe, with all the intuitive fusion that such community implies, and we could no longer entirely escape from one another even if we hated each other's guts and lived at opposite ends of the tier.

19.

Sometimes I think there is only one way to pass unscathed through this maze of tunnels and cages:

To navigate with one's entire nervous system unhooked.

Of the Fittest

Anonymous, Kent GP · 1989

I survive
solely by conforming
to the rules
of those I am
imprisoned with.
Rules that are
harshly enforced.
Deviation from the code
is met with
punishment and
no hope of appeal.
A man's voice
cannot be heard
from a numbered
grave.
I accept this state
outwardly.
Inwardly, I rage
against the injustice.
Yet I dare not
speak out,
for there is
no one to listen.
So I wear
a perpetual mask
and concentrate on
surviving
one more day.

4

THE GUARDS

The modern prison has tried, with very mixed results, to break down the time-entrenched barriers between "us" and "them", the guards and the guarded. Everyone in prison is on guard – this much at least the two groups have in common. John Abbott and M.L. talk about the one-sided nature of the communication between keepers and kept. At the heart of this section is a remarkable series of poems from David Emmonds' collection *Criminal Code*. Emmonds, former LU (Living Unit Officer) at Kent Institution, offers insights which are double-edged in their critical look at both groups. J. Michael Yates, poet and publisher, who has worked at Oakalla and youth detention centres, raises the prison metaphor to a metaphysical speculation yet still anchors it in the experiential: "I have come to know – the complicated way – sanctuary in surroundings of terror." Prison is one of the "numberless steamy windows opening on a nameless metaphor."

Guards Meet the Prisoners

John Abbott · 1985

We sat
stiff
and stared at our feet
while they recited the very minutes.
"Is that alright with you?"
the head suit asked.
Our silence
used to be called dumb insolence
now stilled and acquiescent.
The directive's requirement
for inmate input into decision making
had been fulfilled.

Prison Voltage

It is a closed circuit:
our time
their hallways, the electricity
charges from breaker to capacitor
and back
invisible in the wiring.
Our lightbulb heads glow
with hate.

My Keeper

M.L. · 1986

Soft features,
A concealed weapon
beneath her uniform.
Like a bottle of Johnny Walker Red
to a drunk,
I am gagged
by desire,
bile backing up
and bulging in my throat,
a clogged drain.

A naive schoolboy,
I am confused
by contradictions.

Yet,
neither she
nor I
can escape
her.

I long to hold her,
to clasp her trigger-happy hand.
I want to pound and pummel her.

Like a bored cashier
gazing upon an endless lineup,
she stares past me.
Chastised,
I slink away,
a delinquent mongrel,
and crap under her bed.

the criminal code

David Emmonds · 1987

drinking club
afternoon
strippers
beer
the boys
four blue please
keep the change

and the tattooed hand reaches out
and says thankyou

despite its four fingered elocution of
HATE
the love hand nursing a waiters tray
summered and jail trained arms stating
MOM DAD FTW OUTLAWS RUBY JANET
DEATH BEFORE DISHONOUR

skull and crossbones
playboy bunny
BORN TO DIE
occupying the middle reality
between where he has been
and the final crash site of his desperation
its flight a codified litany

article 306(1)(b) break and enter
you have gate crashed the world

article 303 robbery
you will take what you can get

144 rape
suicide
and not discussed in polite company

and god willing
146 indecent assault
and 169 gross indecency
can be avoided
who cares where the fingers and tongues go
338 the fraud by which
we each must live
326 the pretence to humanity
which gilds us all
312 the criminal possession of pretended emotions
247(2) the unlawful confinement of spirit
319 personation
the escape from self

228 assault with intent
222 attempted murder
218 dont mess with me

the ladder of success
the envy of the underworld

life
twenty five years
a key to the executive washroom
the apple of everyone's intent
case management officers
psychopaths
the parole board
and the rest of the guys
who could only afford the tattoo
FTW
(fuck the world)

serving drinks in afternoon bars
singing the martyrs songs
telling his tale

wistfully

prison exercise yard (summer)

David Emmonds · 1988

the sharks are out tonight
nervous shoal fish dart
parrotfish chatter
gnawing at each other's fins

the whole reef is steaming
under a hunter's moon

crabs hide
and oblivious staghorn
trembles in mysterious currents

huge untouchable groupers
silently fin
dreaming

morays
eyes turned up
slither from crevices
teeth ready
and meat on their minds

barracuda patrol
waiting for the first flash
of scattered scales
or a faint scent of secret blood

day seven

David Emmonds · 1989

it's three in the afternoon
and the last shift is over
day seven as its called
pay cheques are cashed
and its over to the legion
with the rest of the squad

the relief is tangible
translated into hearty laughs
and boisterous behaviour at the bar
as the first pints are ordered

silver handcuff tie pins
and brass pig belt buckles
catch the dim bar lights
ties are loosened
caps have been left on the backseats of cars
a troop of scouts discuss the day's foray
into indian territory

coups are counted
embroidered

and then i fucking told him
strip i said
he just looked at me
but he backed down

fighting all over the place
nasty little bumfuckers
i had the revolver out
if they hadnt stopped

bang
a warning shot anyway

and jim here was in deep shit
right jim
right
three of them ready to go
i just pumped a shell into the shotgun
that sound got their attention
right jim
you bet

what we need in there is more
IN-STANT RE-HAB-IL-IT-ATION

the pints are taking hold
and so is the group propaganda
by five cameraderie is waist deep
shed worries and paranoia
lie around like used lottery tickets

the squad is half ready for day one of the next set
and its actual promise of nothing

Sentences of Treatment and Sentences of Punishment

J. Michael Yates · 1983

The mind swings like the needle of a compass between sentences of treatment and sentences of punishment.

The hand upon the power-saw is undeterred. The alder and fireweed springing back to reclaim what belongs to a wilderness are undeterred.

Everything is winning.

And none.

North is the heaviest judgement of a wilderness upon a mind. Prison is the heaviest judgement on the mind by what a wilderness is not.

Unless the mind consents, whereupon the sense of sentence rearranges itself, and what or who judges vanishes into ice-fog or into white-out or into mist.

At a certain extreme of extremity, all sentences, formal and informal, interchange.

The case does not rest.

Like houses of cards, tall towers of importances collapse and reorganize themselves here.

How one arrives here has little to do with how mainland minds move from one place to another place.

What can be taken for granted – these tones of uncertainty – are not what one takes for granted in the place called "outside".

The ways to die are extraordinary by terms of ordinary lives.

So it is with insular north and with prison. In these places, even the unusual must be approached unusually. For survival, the routine must come to seem extraordinary. Commonplace: the extreme.

I have come to know – the complicated way – sanctuary in surroundings of terror. That a world through the wrong end of the telescope is also a world. That I prefer not to die among the hordes dying of safety.

Certain things can persist only in the languages of what they are not.

Certain things are as they are, like powerlines: held definite only by their bonds, with or without consent.

A north.

A prison.

Mere ideas, therefore not dangerous until expressed. And for a few, not dangerous even then.

Mere forms which feed on the energy of fantasy; therefore delicate and they starve to death easily.

Two of numberless steamy windows opening on a nameless metaphor.

5

WORKING

Prisons try to emulate the work ethic of the world outside the prison walls. However, it is difficult for the inmates to find meaningful work to do in the prison. The *Province* article on the prison printing shop at the B.C. Pen making false documents neatly captures the mixture of the fraudulent and the genuine which characterizes work in prison. The print shop was also used for printing the prisoner publication *Transition* which was an important organ in the development of the penal press in Canada. John Abbott's account of his work stint at Mission speaks for itself. What is striking about work in prisons is that, although the technology has changed, its fundamental role has not changed since its inception. Describing the behaviour of "life men" at the B.C. Penitentiary, the reporter for The *Vancouver Daily World*, January 18, 1892 wrote: "They have become wonderfully mechanical and they know not whether the sun shines or whether it hides behind a cloud. They go about as mere machines, because, in prison at least, it is by far the easiest way to be indifferent to their surroundings." The excerpt from Claire Culhane's *Still Barred From Prison* "Industry and Control," underscores the vital point that the prison business is indeed profitable and is a major employer in the criminal-justice industry. David Emmonds' "guard tower" neatly captures the irony that in the panoptical world of the prison even monitoring play can be work of sorts.

Prison printing shop used for making false documents

The Province · *February 1, 1961*

Guards at the B.C. Penitentiary in New Westminster are keeping a close watch on the prison printing shop since it was revealed that prisoners had been printing false identification papers later used to cash bogus cheques.

Warden Thomas Hall said Tuesday two dies of an official coat of arms were found in the small shop used by inmates for printing the penitentiary magazine *Transition*.

Police in Edmonton are believed to have revealed the scheme when they checked the credentials of a man arrested on a forgery case.

His identification cards showed him to be an inspector of the Federal Department of Justice and an investigator for the Postal Department.

Both cards were printed on glossy stock and bore a coat of arms and photograph.

The card was pulled apart and the glossy side was found to be the back of a photograph. The photograph showed persons watching a soccer game played by the "Penguins."

B.C. Penitentiary has a team known as the Penguins and Warden Hall said prisoners are allowed to buy photographs of games. He said it would be possible for them to stick them together face to face.

Warden Hall said he had no proof the papers were used to cash bogus cheques "but the material would lead one to believe they could be used for that purpose."

The incident occurred before Mr. Hall took over as warden late last year. Warden Hall said the dies were destroyed.

The magazine is now printed every two months instead of monthly, but Warden Hall said that is because of the cost of operating and the difficulty in collecting material.

Reflections On a Short Career In the Mission Prison Factory

John Abbott · 1986

No hope for an industrial machine. The job is never completed. Numbed, calmed in the slow fall. Sargassan curls of routed woodchaff spill off the platform onto the cement. Beds for the Army. Inserted inside: three drawers apiece. Specified maple, jointed, grooved and glued; one size. In a cool, pale grain.

Four hundred and seventy routed edges. One moment, I am robust worker: see how smooth it flows, my hand's smooth motion, the warm grace of natural lines. We are a marvellous creation. At another shuffle, I'm the fool. Robotman. Bobo. Strapped into this blunt choice: a machine the engineers haven't developed a cheaper machine to replace. So I confront my personal worth.

One hundred and twenty-five boards sized and sawed. Motion pared to the efficient. Lift, swing, step, hold, push, lean back, step back, bend, lift. The Dance of the Praying Mantis. Steel toes chafe the fine bones of my feet. It takes all of us to make the factory hum. "How's it goin' John?" Good workers get more jobs. Two hundred and twenty-six beds for the Officers Training Unit – CFB Chilliwack. In CORCAN terminology, there is a private contract. . . .

SandingMaster. We serve you. I place what you expel. Your appetite is involuntary. Your desire mechanical. We, in your service, replace your grit when it is worn. You hum exultant as you grind the grain. Slim sticks, head to head, slip from your vulva, well smoothed. Rubbed wooden shanks, they fall, dry as powder, from my hands. To neat ordered rows. Switch the pallets, and the sticks are pushed through, rubbed smaller, again, until . . . as drawer sides, they slide in frictionless, well fitted, familiar.

"This is a work-oriented institution." The Mission mantra of official faith. "You have been arbitrarily assigned to the factory." Unspoken: the balance of behaviourist controls: Refusal to work is a charge, first conviction (a fine); secondary effects: loss of Private Family Visits, transfers delayed; continued recalcitrance, charge, second conviction (placement in punitive segregation, i.e., the hole, pending negative transfer to a higher security institution). Overhead permanent threat: denial of release, freedom. "Your institutional performance indicates an attitudinal maladjustment. . . ."

A year to pass through the planer. Till I'm smooth as a drawer. The little clock races across the factory floor. Twists past my stiff boots. Orders tumble into the roaring gaps between our earphone silence. Nod like a drill press. Why not obey? Easy and safe. The efficient noise-dampers blank the fierce scream of blade ripping tree flesh. We are muted. Accustomed to the worker's boredom. Prepared for release.

Pour in a calm summer's day.

. . . Autosuck.

The Beltsander. That smell of a dentist drilling teeth. Sense of science boring my head. No pain. Don't care. The silence of "Off." The odor of organic material being worn away. Fill in my frontal lobes with this illusion of mechanical immortality. . . .

By the third day my retreat has become strategic, historic. I skulk behind the machine. Hold my energy close. Scribble these furtive notes. When they can't see, a little tension is off the strings. Urge on the clock like a spectator. Cheat on the minutes. In flight.

Factory Zen. The awareness of consciousness interred by the repetition of the oblivious moment.

Herded to the Buffalo 18 Blower Drillpress. The fourth day of rotation. Mesmerized by the spinning drillbit. The surfaces must be flush. The head of the screw must be below the visible plane. Drillhead anticlockwise; together we reach an apparent stasis in the slow fall of galaxies of dust.

Template change. Reverse slat direction. Spin out the drilled breakthrough splinters. A joke: I've got a ten year sentence as a general helper, 333–23–3E, Cabinet Shop. Four dollars and twenty-five cents Canadian a day. The maximum benefit of my incarceration. One of the criteria for release.

CORCAN: Corrections Canada. CORCAN: their factory unit stamp name. COR CAN COR CAN COR CAN . . .

Push it. Pull it, whines the Dedo blade. Cuts a smooth groove down the center. Adjustable for depth. This time I imagine the demand as exercise: it's a way I can explain it to myself that makes the motion acceptable. The same pallet filled over and over again. With little wooden bodies. Each cycle, another skin removed. A perfect Zen fall into the stack.

The fifth day. Somehow the sandpaper rubbing at this drawer's edge reminds me of wet dog fur. Over my shoulder, the belt sander shines the bones of the drawers, its long ugly tongue racing to a circular eternity. My skin is soft. I am afraid.

Our positions are rotated to correspond to production needs. Hand sanding is a settled task. At its own pace, give or take a few minutes. When you are the entire machine, you don't see the machine. Arborite drawer fronts smoothed every shift.

Flimsy cloth gloves split in the seams baring my fingertips. No one else wears gloves. The less contact I have with the work, the less involved I feel. A little delusion. Breath-masked, face-plated, gloved and earphoned, the immediacy is gone. Like the *Enola Gay* dropping Big Boy from altitude fifteen thousand feet.

The day is sucked up the blowpipes.

It is amazing how silent I have become. I don't talk to anyone. They are the same as me. They sprawl, like I do, on the work during the breaks. They hide in the washroom like I want to. They laugh suddenly in the din and startle me. We have everything in common, but there is no camaraderie, no shared spirit. If I talk, this condition becomes my commodity, and I want to stay a stranger to it.

"Fill in the knotholes and every crack with surfacing putty." Maple coloured. The wood was alive. I am alive. What am I being filled with? "Scrape off the excess, it dries fast, and re-sand." Afterwards they use compressed air to blow off the dust. "If it is done right you can't even see the changes. . . ."

End of shift. "You can go home now," says the fem voice from every corner of the high ceiling. It is not the end of my daze. A supervisor stalks out and corrals several workers. With pink copies of Excellent Performance Notices. The last to quit, the first to start, are rewarded. The hint, unspoken, that they may add up, like good works, to suitability for day parole (parole itself is rarely granted this decade). I stumble out under the sun, glad it hurts. Shift over. . . .

Industry and Control

Claire Culhane · 1985

In searching for an explanation of the rejection of lessons which beg to be learned, we must understand the vital role which the Criminal Justice System (CJS) plays as a part of state control. Bureaucracies generate their own incompetence, and balance their confusion and even self-destruction against the diabolical success with which they prolong the stay of most prisoners, who are essential for the operation of the prison industry. According to Eckstedt and Griffiths in their recent study, *Corrections in Canada: Policy and Practice,* the Correctional Service of Canada (CSC) employs 10,883 people (excluding outside contracts) as part of the CJS, which comprises as well all federal, provincial and municipal courts of law and police forces, and the National Parole Board (NPB). The CJS employs a total of 108,366 people, of whom 17,015, or more than fifteen per cent, hold administrative positions. The 1979 budget of $2.5 billion is estimated to have reached the $3 billion mark.

A further example of prolonging the containment of the "merchandise" is provided in sentence computations. When prisoners query their sentence computations, they can often be provided with three different calculations, of which the "front office" can be depended upon to select the longest period. The 1982–33 annual report of the Correctional Investigator indicates a sharp increase in the number of complaints received regarding "sentence administration" – ninety-seven, compared to a mere (!) sixty-two in 1980–81. Obviously, one way to deal with the serious overcrowding would be to release all those who are serving time beyond their legal release date – a challenge which has never been accepted by any of the CSC specialists.

Before leaving the prisoner-as-merchandise analogy, serious attention must be drawn to the CSC prison industry, known as CORCAN (derived from Corrections Canada). The revenue generated through the sale of CORCAN manufactured goods amounted to $10,308,000 during 1982–83, a 38% increase over 1981–82; and the value of agricultural products produced during 1982–83 was $1,280,000, an increase of 28.5% over 1981–82. The Correctional Service of Canada is restricted to selling goods and services to federal, provincial and municipal governments, and to charitable, religious and non-profit organizations unless special authorization is obtained from the Treasury Board (Solicitor-General's Annual Report, 1982–83).

From a strictly economic viewpoint, prisoners can be viewed as "liabilities" at no small cost to the public – $50,000 per year for each male prisoner and $62,000 for each female prisoner in maximum security. But when considered "assets," this "merchandise" generates hundreds of contracts, thousands of jobs, and millions of dollars in profits – profits which are not realised by the taxpayer but instead remain with CORCAN, the prison industry.

guard tower

David Emmonds · 1988

coils of shining razor wire
shimmer around me
festive

chain link fencing
makes me dizzy
as it kaleidoscopes in hazing heat

sun beats through
the bulletproof shield of my post
in stultifying waves

the radio crackles
with inane messages
and makework

sector nine
scan those inmates
are they really playing softball

my own radio plays country songs
and eagles spill
over the mountains at my back

painful glints of sun
stab off truck roofs
baking in the carpark

i strain my ears
for the first dull sound
of our relief shift

wending through the mountain pass
an hour early as usual
bright as new-made pins

6

DYING

Prisons are about death: from the homicide on the outside which has led to a life sentence on the inside, to the various ways in which inmates die in prison. Tom Elton's "Prison Justice Day" is an "in memoriam" for all those who have died in prison. "The Diver" deals with another way out. Tom Joyce, who taught in the SFU programme at Kent Institution, speaks powerfully in "The Noose" of the bureaucratic post-mortem following a suicide; his "One, two, three" deals succinctly with the ritual of killing in prison. The excerpt from Stephen Reid's novel *Jackrabbit Parole* concerns an assassination at Marion, the Maximum Security Institution in Illinois. Susan Musgrave talks of "state murder," capital punishment, as does Dr. Guy Richmond in the excerpt from his memoir *Prison Doctor*. Richmond's documentary account of a hanging at Oakalla Prison in Burnaby contrasts dramatically with Musgrave's re-creation of the "small celebration in the / prison kitchen afterwards." Capital punishment was outlawed in Canada in 1976; there have been periodic calls for its reinstatement ever since.

Prison Justice Day, August 10th

Tom Elton · 1982

Today we remember our dead,
entering the mind's recesses
where the silver dragons of memory lie
side by side in an uneasy slumber.
We have to know these bodies.

I remember the man
who hung himself with a bedsheet.
He died as his neighbours screamed
in vain for ignoring guards.
They later cut him down, laughing.
They joked about puppets on strings.

So, today we fast and refuse to work,
prefering to stay locked in our cells
– reading books, writing letters,
letting the restless dead
stir to life.

I remember the woman
who carved her flesh with a piece of tin.
Her counsel was herself.
News of her death spread as the red pool swelled,
pushed out beneath her door.

Tonight on the dark tide,
our remembrance grows, calling the other
winged beasts to flight.

The Diver

Tom Elton · 1984

entering prison
on the last day of the year,
is placed in a cell
that is to be his home
for the rest of his life.

No one talks to the diver.
We are resting
for the traditional night of noise and
the quiet of the block is broken
only by an occasional word,
the sound of a cup set down, the
echoing crash as a toilet flushes.

On the windows in front of the cells,
I can see the diver's reflection:
prone on his bunk,
hands folded behind his head –
he is staring at the ceiling.

It is almost twelve; we prepare
for the advent. Hands grip steel
mugs, tin cans, sticks – anything
that will make a noise
when banged against the bars.

Midnight. Out on the Fraser River
boats whistle shrilly.
Our cell bars shed their paint
as we bang and scream.

Hundreds release their rage.
Hours pass. We tire, hands cramp
and blister, voices go hoarse.
One by one we drop from the mass until,
some time around three,
the block is cloaked in silence.

Morning, and the cell doors open.
We on "high five" file down the tier
to the kitchen for our trays.
The diver asks his neighbour: are all
nights like that?
and gets his answer in an affirmative nod
by a man who continues on –
ignoring the diver

knifing though the air
to the cement pool below.

One, two, three

Tom Joyce · 1982

It takes three to take a life:
one to keep watch, one to hold
and one to work the knife.

Noose

Hermetic in its plastic cell
discarded among the dolours
of memos, slabs of bald paper
obscure logarithms and drab
letters from one bored official
to another re: pay scale, study
report, just another item of office
furniture really, this simple
four foot stretch of white canvas
mere inches across, once taut
speckled with blood, now dull
passive, flattened in its plastic:
evidence I touch inadvertently
among the pages on the desk, and
in the moments that it takes to die
a man like purple beef strangles
beneath my finger.

The Killing

Stephen Reid · 1986

It was almost Christmas before the first killing came. Noon hour. C-unit was emptied. They were serving mystery meat for lunch and I decided to skip. I was sitting out on the bottom range at a card table teaching a cowboy from Montana how to play cribbage. He didn't like mystery either.

"Fifteen-six, fifteen-eight. My game Bobby. That's five cartons you owe me." Damned cowboy learned fast too. He went for a piss.

Stillborn Louie appeared quietly at my elbow.

"Hello, Louie."

He grunted and gestured to the pack of Camels on the table. I gave him one. They belonged to the cowboy, but seeing as how I was buying. . . .

Stillborn Louie never spoke. He was a small guy and his bones poked under his clothes. He had eyes that bulged white and a jaw that was always dirty. Stillborn Louie had been here so long he had forgotten why.

Five cons from another unit came through the hall doors, moving in single file, full of deadly purpose. The guard at the desk jumped up to halt the unauthorized entry but the lead man threw down on him with a knife the length of a centurion's sword. The other four continued on. With the keys.

Stillborn Louie ducked into the mop room. The cowboy was back, monitoring me into my chair. "Sit there." He spoke low and harsh. "This is not our business."

I heard the lock on the end grille. Stared down at the card in my hand. It was the King of Clubs.

They marched by. Didn't break stride, didn't look our way. Black boots with pant legs tucked in. Black gloves. Knitted skull caps. Four soldiers.

The procession turned into cell 11. The last man in line swung around sharply, planted his feet, and stayed outside the cell. The doorman.

I heard a small scuffle of feet. A choked cry. A long silence.

Then the stabbing began. First the sound of one knife, like a trowel being plunged into wet cement, the sucking sound of its retreat. Then a whole lot of trowels plunging and sucking. It went on too long. The card curled in my hand.

The sounds stopped, and three men filed out, the sentry stepping into his place at the rear. As the column left the range, each man in turn laid his knife down on the desk and walked out the door like they were going off shift. The last soldier released the guard and followed suit. I unlock my fist and the King of Clubs fell to the table, never to be played again.

The guard at the end of the range pushed the deuces button and tried to make sounds like he was giving orders around here. It was feeble.

The victim lurched out of cell 11 and sprawled along the handrail like an exhausted athlete. He wore an awkward smile as if he were embarrassed for making such a scene. Too freshly butchered, he didn't know enough to be dead.

The cowboy handed him a lit Camel. The cigarette dangled from his lips and he tried to look cool, as if to say he'd had closer shaves than this before. The guy was dead before the ash became a problem.

Stillborn Louie picked the cigarette from the guy's lips and pinched off the coal. There was a white spot where a small piece of paper had stuck to his bottom lip – then blood gushed over it and the body slumped on its side.

Guards were everywhere. We were shoved up against a wall.

"No! No! Not them! They were just playing cards!" The two-minute hostage cleared us of any part in it.

Cameras flashed, the body was removed, the assassins were taken to the hole, and Montana had mopped up the blood before the rest of the cell block returned from lunch. Stillborn Louie relit the cigarette, and I went back to my cell on the second tier. I lay on my bunk and closed my eyes but the sucking sounds didn't stop. I missed supper too.

Due Process

Susan Musgrave · 1988

So there was this
small celebration in the
prison kitchen afterwards,
with doughnuts and
well-laced coffee and
idle talk of the last
double-noose ceremony.

One of the boys took seventeen minutes
to die. The other,
twenty-three. They fell together
without a sound
though you could see from their eyes
they had been weeping recently.

They say a good hangman
is hard to find;
a good man is even harder.

Hobbled out, prayed over
trussed bagged noosed and dropped

strangulation completes the process
sooner or later.

The Pound of Flesh

Dr. Guy Richmond · 1975

Attendance at executions was the duty I dreaded most and it is curious that in times of stress I have recurrent dreams of an execution. Sometimes I had known the condemned men long before they committed murder. The devastating period between sentence, appeal and execution placed an intolerable strain on the condemned person. Temporary staff members were called in to cover the twenty-four-hour supervision of the death tier. Some of these elderly men were of comfort to the occupants and formed helpful relationships. A heavy share of the burden was carried by the doctor and the Chaplain who was of very great assistance in the sad months, weeks, days and hours before execution. There was hope of reprieve right up to the end, though the condemned man was told of the cabinet's decision a day or so prior to execution. It was the custom of the government to delay transmitting the decision until close to the appointed day, so that hope for a reprieve was kept alive as long as possible, and a telephone line was kept open up to the moment of hanging just in case Ottawa changed its mind. I paid frequent visits to the condemned men from the time they were sentenced, and with the one exception I have always admired their courage and the seeming composure with which they met their deaths. I was entrusted with many confidences which will never be divulged. I especially recall the thoughtfulness of one man who was so anxious, just before he was hanged, that someone should drive his elderly minister home after the execution.

I saw much of the condemned man during his last day. Usually I went home early for an hour or two in the afternoon. On my return in the evening of one of these occasions I drove through the gate on my way to pay a call at the Women's Building before going to the condemned tier. This meant driving past a row of trees within view of the condemned. As I was passing the trees, I noticed some birds in them and thought that among them I saw a flash of blue. We had lost a budgie from the T.B. ward and I wondered if this was he. So I stopped and walked to the trees where the birds were but I couldn't see our budgie. I went to the women's section, then on to the condemned tier. I could see at once that

Eddie was especially agitated.

"Has the hangman arrived?"

"Yes," I replied, "I think so. Have you any special reason for asking?"

"I was scared. I saw you looking at a tree and thought you were choosing a branch for me."

"Of course I wasn't. I was looking for a lost budgie!" I explained.

By that time the executioner had completed his rehearsal and as usual I made of point of going to his room to tell him a little about the man he was to hang, so that if at all possible he would regard him more as a person rather than just a potential corpse. There was a language barrier which made communication difficult, but I managed as best I could. He appeared utterly unconcerned. It was just a job, at which he was skilled.

Unless there is careful calculation of the drop required for height and weight of the victim, and unless the noose is in the correct position around the neck, there may be ghastly consequences such as decapitation or prolonged suffering. In each case I was concerned to know whether the death had occurred by strangling only or whether there had been in addition a more sudden and certain loss of sensation and vital functions by fracture of one of the cervical vertebrae, so after the hanging we x-rayed the neck with a portable machine. Death by fracture of one or more of the cervical vertebrae would hopefully lessen the agony. In no case was the radiologist who examined the films able to report such a fracture, or indeed a dislocation, though there was some stretching.

The execution was at midnight and I paid my final visit to the condemned cell at 11 P.M. The Chaplain was there but I wanted to say good-bye.

"I'm sorry to interrupt, Padre, but I just wanted to tell Eddie that he'll be getting his shot in a few minutes. It'll make you feel a bit more comfortable, Eddie, but it won't knock you out."

"Will you be there, Doc?"

"Yes, of course."

"You'll make sure I'm dead, won't you?"

"Yes, I promise."

"Bye, Doc, thanks for everything."

"Bye for now, Eddie. God bless."

I shook hands and sadly went up to my office where I sat quietly. The whole prison was deathly still; I had left orders for mild sedation to be given to anyone who was restless and asked for attention.

The hand of the clock crept on. One of the hospital staff had come in specially to be with me at the foot of the drop. 11:30 P.M. and he would be giving Eddie his shot. Time to go down.

"Everything all right, Mr. Seymour? I'll be sleeping here tonight. Make me up a bed in the workers' ward, will you?" Then I went down to the basement part of the gaol, through the clothing storage rooms. There was a smell of moth balls, and ever since their odour has distressed me. I walked to the end of one of these rooms where there was a stretcher on the floor covered with a clean white sheet. The door of what looked like a large cupboard was open. It was dark except for a faint chink of light way up high, filtering through the crack between the two floors of the drop.

I could hear the sound of people assembling in the execution chamber, the Warden and his attending staff, the coroner and his jury, and other invited guests. I looked at my watch . . . 11:55. I paced up and down the room, as I used to in an air raid waiting for the next bomb to fall, the same dry mouth, the same excretion of adrenalin, the same thumping heart. There was silence now up above. It was midnight. I stepped back into what used to be the base of an elevator shaft. I could hear footsteps approaching the drop. Then a shuffling sound. I knew Eddie was wearing slippers. A pause while the hood was being placed on him and then the straps and noose. Then I heard the hangman pull the lever, followed by a clanging thud as the sections of the drop hit the walls. Two slippers dropped at my feet. The hospital officer stooped to pick them up. I could hear the creak of the pulley as Eddie was lowered low enough for me to listen to his heart with my stethoscope. The rope was quivering. His legs rose in spasm and dropped again. I opened his shirt and listened. His heart was beating rapidly, 120, 130, 140, 150 . . . then racing, becoming weaker and irregular. Fainter, fainter, 6, 7, 8, minutes since the drop, 10 minutes, not a sound, absolute stillness. I turned to the officers and recorded the death as 12:13 a.m. The body was lowered to the ground. By now the hangman was there to cut the rope and remove the noose, hood and straps. There were deep groves around the neck and friction burns. Eddie was laid reverently on the stretcher and covered with a sheet; the eyes were closed and the tongue pressed back into the mouth.

My final duty was to sign the document which was to be posted at the prison gate announcing that as "prison surgeon" I had pronounced Eddie dead.

So another tragedy had been enacted. I went up to the infirmary to have a cup of coffee with the officers on duty and then to bed but not to sleep, only to relive the events of the last several hours. The other occupants of the ward were sound asleep.

7

SURVIVING

This section moves from the dramatic impact of death to the mundane acts of survival which can be heroic in themselves. John Abbott's "The Complete Angler" makes this point, along with the rider that these fantasy escapes contain their own dangers. The body and the mind conspire in the psychosomatic "prison sickness" of Clyde Kennedy's "Let it R.I.P." Kennedy's story was published posthumously in *Prison Journal* 8 (1989). On December 25, 1988 Kennedy, who was paroled at a half-way house, drove a truck off the pier at Blaine, Washington. His body was never recovered and only his Bible was found in the vehicle. Kenny Cound's "Time Is a Pecker" concerns itself with similarly deviant ways in which to kill time. His manuscript was found in a wastepaper basket at Kent Institution's Academic Centre, where it was salvaged by John Abbott. "The Palimpsest" (our choice of name for this untitled work) focuses on the strategies employed by a man in the hole so that he can manage to count off the days to Christmas – the "time cancer" theme that runs through all these works in this section.

The Complete Angler

John Abbott · 1984

He is an expensive friend
who throws the lures,
the one who spins those light expansive dreams,
of power,
when we're in such a powerless position,
in prison.

I longed that his eyes not gleam
so yacht rich and palm shadowed
of those young Thai girls he will adopt
to rub in his every whim
when he is let out.

Scuba diving down the coral reefs,
Not dead but living stones
he says, the rainbowed fish
are tame to touch,
we only spear what we can eat
beside the fire, the celluloid night,
with those careless girls between us.

The track around the yard runs licking fingertips
to Sugar Loaf mountain and tropical kisses:
Out there it only rains at night
and the native message is a polygamous ancient art.
He smiles past me as the colours flash by.

Remember not the tear of the hook in our gums,
the shud of the club on the back of a slick head,
the breath starved frenzy
pinioned in the gillnet.

He means to soothe me, signalling quietly
Forget, Forget,
He is an expensive friend because he has bought all of his dreams.

Let it R.I.P.

Clyde Kennedy · 1988

It was the influenza that was responsible for some of it. That elusive virus that invaded the body and induced feverish chills and nausea: an insidious disease for which none had yet found a sure-fire cure, or cause for that matter. Sure, they called it a virus, all those eminent doctors and scientists, but then they called almost every inexplicable illness a virus these days.

He rolled over onto his side upon his small cot and shuddered involuntarily. His brow dripped beads of cold sweat and he had grown tired of wiping himself dry with his towel which was now drenched as damp as most of his body. "The worst of it was over now at any rate," he thought. Surely after five days it was bound to break, to let up. That was the law of nature.

"But then what would I know about the law of nature," he exclaimed suddenly, pushing aside the covers and leaping unsteadily to his feet. "Criminal laws are another story," he muttered, staring at the enormous bars securing the window of his cell. They were huge. Five inches in diameter. Iron bars; but none can see the irony but me he mused, smiling wryly. "A cell is a cell," he thought, but with this flu business things were different somehow. His perspective had fled him and he loathed himself because of it.

He recalled his visit to the nursing station the day before yesterday. After submitting the usual request application seeking medical attention, he now wondered if his wording on the form had been appropriate.

"I demand immediate attention for cancer," he had written. He knew that they had probably raised their medical eyebrows over that one and he laughed at the thought. A regular deputy dawg laugh. It had become part of his nature. A "characteristic" the psychologist would have termed it. An idiosyncracy. "This man has a deputy dawg laugh originating somewhere deep within his inherently devious nature!" Oh, he could imagine them writing that down all right. Why it was probably buried in a report somewhere in his file right at this very moment.

Away off in the distance a train whistle wailed. Once, twice. Silence.

He imagined a cumbersome castiron one-eyed monster sliding over the tracks to places unknown. The whistle was routine. In the afternoon, late at night and again very early in the morning, it wailed. Anonymous routine. Briefly he considered labelling it with a name. "The Monster," he thought. That seemed apt. Suddenly he felt very ill and staggered to the corner of the cell where he vomited toward the toilet, spewing forth a green bilish liquid. Feeling faint he weakly pushed the flush button of the commode and meandered unsteadily back to his cot and reclined with the rumbling sound of foul smelling fluid resounding away from the drain.

He ignored the ice cold of his steel framed cot where it seared into his bare flesh like a hot fire brand and he thought about his trip to the nursing station. The prison guards had come for him with hand-cuffs, shackling him securely before leading him from the cell. They seemed nervous. Outside in the open air the blasts of frigid wind seemed to blow right through his feverish body as he weaved a weary path across the courtyard. It seemed an eternity before they reached the inner sanctum of the nursing station. He sat waiting on the hard wooden bench wondering why he had bothered to come. There was no real treatment available here he only knew too well. There was no resident doctor. Just a handful of nursing staff who appeared to be even more incompetent than the administrative officials of the penitentiary. "One could die waiting," he thought. Some had, interminably waiting.

When the nurse finally appeared she was wearing white plastic gloves and a blue face mask covering her mouth and nose, held in place by a slim elastic band. She was fiftyish and her hair was streaked with gray in patches as though it had been dabbed on with a paint brush. She led him into the examination room. The guards stood fidgeting at the entrance of the doorway.

"Kelly?" she mumbled sternly from behind the mask.

"No, it's Collins," he replied.

"Number?"

"235055A," he responded.

"You've claimed to have AIDS," she continued harshly.

"AIDS!" he exclaimed, interjecting quickly. "Who said that? I have cancer and the flu as well."

She seemed more relieved suddenly and her entire demeanour changed as she removed the facial mask.

"Well we will have to do some blood-work and x-rays. For verification of course."

"Oh it's not that type of cancer," he said casually, enjoying the charade by now, though he was sweating profusely, "It's the other kind."

"What other kind?" she asked in obvious exasperation, frowning in his direction.

"The other kind," he replied, "Prison cancer. Cancer of the mind. Cancer of the spirit. It's not treatable as far as I know. There's other names for it I guess. I used to think it was pure unadulterated hate, but it's more than that. Me, I just call it Prison cancer. In fact I diagnosed myself," he continued, rambling on now, scarcely conscious of what he was saying or where his dialogue was headed. "The cancer I can live with. There's not much physical pain; just a quiet sort of numbness that spreads and grips you with . . ."

"Alright, that's enough of that kind of talk now," she yelled, motioning to the two guards with flailing hands. "Get him out of here!"

The flu persisted although he could sense its presence abating somewhat. Stretched out on his cot he pulled the covers over him. He knew it was almost that time. The death parade. The killing time. It was his daily routine. He dreaded the thought of his condition interfering with one of his few simple pleasures. He had three of them to do today. Four, including the nurse. He would start with her. He strove for determination beneath the covers. It would be messy as always. Particularly the dismembering. He would enjoy flushing the evidence away down the toilet as always. It was routine of course. Imaginary routine. Why, how else could they expect a man with prison cancer to get by? He knew they understood.

Time Is a Pecker

Kenny Cound · 1983

Kenny was given a cell. He was amazed at the cleanliness of the place, except for a small piece of meat on his desk. It looked very fresh. This was not included in the preconception he had had of prison – but he knew the hygiene was all a facade because of the filthy degradation he had witnessed all around him on his way in. He read it in the eyes and gestures of the other convicts. I guess, he thought, that must be the way that the authorities would like to portray the place. He shrugged, well it is just a place to do time. First step was to find some imaginative way to gauge it by.

Let me see, he thought. There is slow time, fast time, good time – nice weather, bad weather. The Indians had a good way to gauge time. When things happened they would refer to that time as, for instance, the time the chief's horse died or the year of the big snow. I see, he thought, that they serve time here as a piece of meat. The significance of this overwhelmed him. What is a piece of meat but dead flesh. But there was a clock on the wall just by his head and it was inhibiting him from thinking clearly. It sounded like there was a woodpecker in that clock. With the constant pecking sound cracking at his head, he thought, I'm going to need some imagination. That pecking sound might be a woodpecker pecking away at my imagination. I'll have to go see what the other convicts do with their time. I've got to move quickly because, if I find out that that woodpecker is really pecking away at my imagination, I'll have to find some way to free it before it goes to pieces altogether.

So Kenny went to check out what kinds of imagination he could find. He asked one guy lifting weights if the pecking sound in the clock could be a woodpecker pecking away at his imagination. The convict replied that it couldn't be because his imagination was too big to fit in that small a box. This was confirmed by several other convicts standing around who guffawed and said they had imaginations of great magnitude too.

But this did not satisfy Kenny because he was sure that the monotonous clicking had to have some kind of effect upon his power to fantasize.

So he went back to his cell to look at the time that lay before him. The piece of meat was getting green around the edges. This depressed him a bit so he went to see a neighbour about how he dealt with it. He visited a man in the next cell who had been studying time for the last seventeen years. He asked him what he should do.

"Well", the man said, "Me, I watch it and when it turns green around the edges like that, I slice the green parts off and toss them in that bucket over there – Like this! And he quickly sliced off the green edges. The meat was smaller but it was red again.

"Where does it go from there? " Kenny asked.

"Oh, to the dump," was the only reply he received. Well, there ain't much to be learned here, he thought and he left.

Kenny was still sure that the clicking sound in the clock was being fed by his imagination. If it wasn't, then why was he feeling so bored and uninspired? Sometimes he felt like just tearing it off the wall and seeing what answers were inside. But he was afraid that if he did that he might break something and he wouldn't be able to put it back together again.

So one morning, before he woke up, he went for a stroll down the walkway where he met a guy he knew was just hanging around playing the duck. Previously they had had some weird conversation in which he had convinced the guy he was a nutbar.

"Hi," he said, "Nice to see you out this morning so early. See all the zombies. Let's have some fun with them. No. Don't go. Stay with us". Kenny was with a friend and they seemed to be joined at the wrists. He got afraid suddenly. "No way! Maybe it's best I just pretend I'm a zombie too and get away from these guys. Well at least he had got an answer to one thing: If you've got a friend who can make you believe that what you are doing is imaginative, then you've got some kind of imagination – Sadly it was not the kind he was looking for however. So he woke up and convinced himself that it was a dream and that a new piece of meat was waiting on his table to be worked on. Anyway, it wasn't going to take that long for this piece of meat to go green because the sun was out today, shining directly on it. He turned another thought over in his mind: If there was some kind of way to preserve the meat, it might give the clock more time and possibly drive that woodpecker nuts, if it didn't drive him nuts first. But that remained to be seen. Kenny got out his pen and started to section the meat off. The constant pecking at the back of his head went on as usual and it kind of made him wonder about life. What was the lifespan of a woodpecker? It must be shorter than a man's. All he had to do was outlast that woodpecker and make sure he never let it escape so it could reproduce.

Palimpsest

Anonymous · 1953

The palimpsest below appeared in the December 1953 edition of Transition. *It was censored by the B.C. Penitentiary Administration and was overprinted with "MERRY CHRISTMAS" to conserve paper. What follows is the decoded version:*

Thirteen of the fourteen cells in the confinement block were unoccupied. The sprawled form of a sleeping man covered the wooden bunk of the one cell in service. He slept as though accustomed to the punishment of a plank paillasse.

The muted echo of a struck bell drifted down the tunnel connecting the Hole to the Main Dome of the penitentiary. Behind a square of murky glass set flush with the ceiling an entombed bulb suddenly glowed with electric life. It was a feeble light that the area could face without flinching but it was strong enough to awaken the sleeping man.

Slowly, so as not to disturb the sleep stupor that still cradled him, he rolled over onto his back. His eyes opened and as quickly retreated

SORRY FOLKS, you won't be able to read these two pages. We got ahead of ourselves and ran off a story that shouldn't have gone.

Since we operate on the edge of bankruptcy at all times, and had the story mimeoed on two pages and some 1500 sheets of paper, we couldn't afford to throw the work away. To make the blotted out story a little less of an eyesore, we changed the color and concealed the plot. It won't happen again, we hope!

behind the sheltering awning of lids. Almost mechanically his hands fumbled at the folded jacket under his head. Awakened nerves were being reminded that an unpadded board makes an uncomfortable bed.

Suddenly the figure convulsed with life. He pushed himself into a sitting position. Rubbing the sleep from his eyes he swung his feet to the floor. His thin drawn features, set in a sleepy scowl, began to relax. A smile of anticipation erased the lines of hunger.

This is it! he exulted silently. This is it!

His eyes turned to the wall to check his improvised calendar. There, amid the myriad initials and cancelled box scores of days dedicated to enforced diets was his own record of time served. The metal tip of his shoe lace had scored the count of meal-less days in the concrete. Slowly he counted the scratches. His fingers tolled them off. One, two, three . . . eight . . . fifteen . . . eighteen, he tallied the eighteen hungry days. The total reassured him.

That's right. I was sentenced to twenty-one days on the seventh he mused. This has to be it.

Turning to the sink he splashed the sleep out of his face with cold water. For once it didn't bother him. It was Christmas. He was going to eat.

Man, am I ever glad they relax the rules in the Hole at Christmas, he exulted. I might make myself sick on the rich food but to hell with it. I'm going to gorge myself anyway. Let me see, what did we get for Christmas last year at breakfast? Oh yeah, I remember. We got shredded wheat, bacon and eggs, hot buns, honey and special made coffee. Or did we get two desserts? Sure, we got sliced peaches as well as honey.

Thinking of that memorable meal revived the long harnessed hunger in his body. The self-imposed discipline that normally denied recognition to his craving for food snapped. His stomach growled and knotted in a practice convulsion of digestion. The saliva slopped in his mouth. But it was a pleasant pain.

Tucking his folded jacket under his head for a pillow he stretched out on the plank bunk. His eyes stared into the anemic light. He stared and saw only peaches, big unblemished blobs of golden fruit blanketed in amber syrup. When that picture faded it was replaced by the guilty eyes of fried eggs staring at him from a collar of crisp bacon.

A key grated in a lock. The echo of anticipation intensified. He heard the shuffle of feet on concrete in the distance. In his mind he visualized the unseen action. The guard bringing his breakfast had unlocked the main barrier and was walking through the tunnel.

The vision of a heaped tray grew vivid.

The boys in the kitchen know it's for the hole so they'll really load it up, he reminded himself gloatingly.

He heard the shuffle of feet near the end of the tier, then silence.

He imagined the rasp of a pen on paper. He knew the guard had to sign in.

The silence deepened. He found himself tensing. His ears echoed the beat of his heart. A curse of impatience welled in his throat. Hunger churned his stomach.

When the guard finally stirred into motion he was limp with excitement.

He relaxed, weakly allowing himself the last pleasurable spasm of anticipation. Each footstep brought the bacon and eggs closer. With closed eyes he inhaled their delectable aroma. The taste lay heavy on his tongue.

"Here grab this!"

Opening his eyes to the gruff command he saw four slices of bread being thrust through the bars at him.

"What's this?" he stammered, "You're supposed to get a regular meal at Christmas even if you are in the Hole," he added half hysterically.

"Christmas?" the guard returned with a humouring smile, "What's the matter, you blowing your top? Christmas isn't until tomorrow."

8

THE WOMEN

Prisons do not, of course, only enclose those who are physically incarcerated there; in their wake are families, loved ones, friends . . . J.E. Telfer's lead essay, and her poems which conclude this section, concentrate on these "lost ones" and how they deal with the consequences of imprisonment. Our prisons are designed for men; there is only one Federal Prison for Women (P4W in Kingston). Diana Hartley writes from Lakeside Correctional Centre, the women's prison annexed to Oakalla; 15-year-old Evelyn Lau writes about her stay in a youth detention centre. Janet Urquhart taught ABE (Adult Basic Education) for Fraser Valley College at Kent Institution and "Dragon's Teeth" talks of her experiences there. For most women, prison is a place they visit to see their men. Susan Musgrave's poems discuss Millhaven Penitentiary in Ontario where she met Stephen Reid while she was writer-in-residence at Waterloo University. She also writes about Kent Institution where Reid was transferred and where they were married in 1987. Lloyd Moffat's "Your Voice," the only piece by a man in this section, testifies to how the voice of the woman keeps him going at the same time that it is inextricably intertwined with the chains and "some silent concrete / that was waiting / for both of us."

The Forgotten Women

J. E. Telfer · 1985

They pass by unnoticed in a crowd, unless,perhaps, one has an eye for a certain indefinable sadness. They are, however, different from most women: they are the wives and lovers of men incarcerated behind penitentiary walls. They are as oppressed and imprisoned in their own fashion as the men that they love.

Today's society devotes much media coverage to its popular ailments. Drugs, alcohol, child abuse, wife battering, venereal diseases, sexual discrimination and women's rights all receive much needed attention. Countless individuals specialize in each of these fields, and while these problems still exist, vast amounts of government and private funding and inestimable labour hours are making progress in all of these areas. Prisoners themselves are often the focus for television specials and talk shows, but their women are still forgotten.

We are out here, isolated and alienated, yet still within society. There is a trend in our judicial system towards imprisoning more men for lengthier sentences, so our numbers also increase.

What does a man's life sentence mean to the woman left behind on the street? It means learning how to be strong and patient. It means fighting against the mockery that the system has created of your marriage, of your whole life. It means changing your entire manner of existence.

The majority of prisons are deliberately constructed somewhere in rural obscurity. If we hide them all the way from view, everybody will be able to forget that they're even there. The crimes, the criminals and their families, however, were generally bred of the big city, so there the wives remain. If they are employed, transfer to the country is unlikely. To visit their husbands they must find the time to fit into the prison visiting schedule and then travel expensive distances to see their spouse an average of twice a week, four hours for your marriage out of every 168 hours. If that seems an impossible situation for her, the wife can relocate to the prison area and see her husband four different days of the week for a total of ten hours. From the marital standpoint, the latter would most certainly seem the preferable choice. But at what cost?

The government picks up this tab. They now need support not only the convict, but his wife and children. Welfare is the name of this game. Even for the educated and skilled, the possibilities for employment in a small rural community, especially in the economic climate of today, are slim to none. And we are here for a long stay.

Since visits do not usurp much of our time, and we have no jobs, we spend much of the time at home. We are presented with the unavoidable opportunity of getting to know our neighbors. In a small prison town, where the major sources of employment are the prisons and the RCMP station, many of our neighbours are staff members from those places. The antipathy between "us" and "them" doesn't make for open warfare, but it does create a broad rift throughout the community. Definitely not an ideal residential situation, brimming over as it is with prejudice and paranoia. So we exist within our own apartment/cells, alone with our thoughts.

We have a great deal to ponder. With the initial "pinch" we began an extended trek through the stages of grief, similar to that which one experiences upon the demise of a loved one. We, too, suffer the phases of shock, denial, anger, mourning and acceptance.

The initial shock encompasses all the trauma of having your spouse forcibly and physically separated from you by a will outside of your own and his. It is a fact as irrevocable and unchangeable as death itself. Reality abruptly becomes highly unpleasant and most painfully difficult to face. The impact of this shock reveals itself in such responses as a general mental stupor, severe depression, memory dysfunction, and symptoms such as sudden bouts of the shakes. The part that is really scary, but you don't realize it until months/years later, is that you actually believe at the time that you're functioning quite satisfactorily and nearly normally.

After the major shock at the beginning is working its way through, you find the denial phase starting. You can't imagine how you will be able to cope with your husband in jail; therefore, this can't possibly be occurring in your life. It simply isn't true that your husband is imprisoned, separate from you. Finally some back portion of the mind speaks up and impresses cold reality upon your conscious mind.

But it isn't right, it just isn't right! Anger flares, bright, hot and all-consuming. Your indignation and outrage (righteous or not) at how unjust a place this world is, how your life is now in such terrible turmoil, and how circumstances are so far beyond your power to change engulf every fibre of your being. You hate, in a purer form than ever previously within your experience. Your hatred is directed everywhere: at the "System" (*i.e.* cops, judges, prosecutors, and even media reporters), at every person that you encounter, at your spouse, at yourself and your god. Your applecart has not only been overturned, but enormous boots have stomped it flat, and you resent and hold everyone and everything absurdly accountable.

Eventually comes the ultimate realization that we have been the sole authors of our own fates, not mere victims of the system, and that our present positions are only the inevitable outcomes of our own and our spouses' ill-considered actions.

Enter now the mourning, the soul-wrenching sadness. We grieve for all that is lost of our previous pleasures of daily existence; we shed tears for the long years to come. The future has ceased to be an optimistic prospect: it looms with empty days and wasted time. Our sorrow is for ourselves, our husbands, and for our relationships which we fear will be the next fatality in this tragic scenario. In many cases this is the result.

Finally, at long last, we reach the relief of acceptance. The anger and the sorrow are no longer felt with such tortuous intensity. The boggled, confused brain has now come to the bitter awareness that the repeated blows of imprisonment, conviction, sentence, and lost appeal are indeed real. Our husbands will be in prison for a very long time. If we are to continue our marriages, our entire lives will be fraught with unusual stresses and strains. And before we can have a future together with our husbands in that magical state we call freedom, we have many years of waiting ahead.

We have not existed in a vacuum on the street: husband and wife have parents, siblings, and other relatives, all of whom are affected. Their reactions in turn affect us.

A not unusual reaction for the husband's family is to view the wife as their burden-reliever. The primary support person for the man will be his wife, and many of his family may decide that they need not visit or correspond with any frequency. Their feelings of guilt are absolved by assuring themselves that his wife will "look after him." Virtual abandonment of the man by his family is a further hardship upon him and his wife.

The wife's family is less likely to be sympathetic to the man's situation. Reactions vary, but can include a stance of non-support as long as the woman remains in the relationship. This can place the woman in the untenable position of feeling compelled to make an either/or choice between her parents and her husband. Most certainly this is an impossible choice to have to make, which adds still another needless stress.

The woman is now the emotional mainstay for her husband, but she also is desperately in need of support herself, especially at the beginning. The presence of a close friend is invaluable, someone who is non-judgemental, patient, tolerant, who will listen but say little, and who can assist in the simple day-to-day tasks of living. Fortunately, this extremely needy stage is quite short-lived.

In an attempt to interact with people who can really understand her problems, the wife further isolates herself by associating with other "joint broads," often to the exclusion of other friendships. In seeking compassion and understanding, she actually extends her feelings of alienation. Together, these women, all struggling in similar situations, can share their problems and some solutions. They can let off steam, bitch, rant and rave with women who can appreciate their frustrations. Other friends often cannot conceptualize the predicament. Within the confines of these kinds of "joint" relationships, we are able to display some of our vulnerability and share our secret fears and anxieties.

First and foremost is the awful dread that one day the notification will arrive that the husband is dead. It is a fear with which we all must live, each and every day of the sentence. We hear of it happening to others, and we carry the knowledge that it can happen anytime, for any or no reason. In prison, some men kill; some men are killed. It is really very simple, and in its simplicity lies its terror.

The flip side is knowing that life inside, with the unique codes and morals of that separate reality, implies also that one day the man whom we love may be in a position where he must kill another human being. The moral and religious feelings surrounding that possibility create deep fears in themselves. On another level, we must live with the knowledge that if that possibility comes to pass, we will have to face the loss of the chance of a future parole, and the termination of all hope for a life together on the street.

Continually we fear for our husband's health. A serious injury or illness for the average citizen can rapidly become a terminal one for someone inside prison walls. Medical facilities are limited and inadequate to contend with anything of major consequence. Even if a suitable diagnosis is made in enough time, the patient is still located in a rural area. He must be "rushed" to a city centre for further treatment, battling government red tape. So we wonder: will he get there in time? Once again we can only wait helplessly.

Less dramatic, but of more day-to-day concern, is the fear that the husband may be found guilty of transgressing an institutional rule, unwittingly, unavoidably, or deliberately. He might even be charged for an offence as a result of an unearned accusation. The repercussions can be severe for us, such as being placed on screened (telephone) visits, being barred from group open house events, having private family visits (PFVS) cancelled or even having husbands transferred to another distant prison or Special Handling Unit. Our visits are privileges; they are not rights. So as they are given, so may they also be taken away. The donkey and the carrot are high-profile residents at any penal institution.

The woman fears that she, too, may contravene some rule and that that may produce the same results. Exercise of self-control and good judgement when visiting the institution and while dealing with the staff members with whom she must come in contact is critical to the continuation of her visiting privileges. She also comes into jeopardy of losing her visits should she be less than a model citizen in her "street" life. Any kind of criminal charge (prior to trial and verdict, although she may be found innocent) will result in screened visits only, no open houses, no private family visits. The woman carries considerable responsibility on her own shoulders for maintaining acceptable behavior for the continuation of the various visiting privileges.

With all the pain, stress and fear, there are some compensating times available to some of us, brief, albeit, but respites of a kind from doing time. These twilight zone periods are officially designated the private family visits. Whatever we may say about them on the negative side, very few of us would willingly trade them for anything.

PFVS provide an opportunity for the convict and his wife, or other members of his immediate family, to be together continuously for between 24 and 72 hours, in a relatively normal setting. In two-bedroom mobile homes, they can cook, eat, talk, play, enjoy music or television, sleep and make love. The couple can converse at any length they choose in an environment which the propaganda claims to be unmonitored. Not that they want to discuss criminal activity, past, present or future, but like all families, they prefer that certain matters remain private. Such privacy is not possible during the electronic monitoring and recording of regular visits.

In the trailer we have the precious privacy to disagree. It seems ludicrous that married adults should not be able to argue together (a psychologically healthy behavior), but when your time together is spent almost exclusively in a small visiting room with eleven or so other couples, in a setting reminiscent of a grade school classroom with several teachers omnipresent, your disagreements are of necessity so low-key as to be almost humorous. Raised voices and profane language would interfere with the visits of the other couples and would likely endanger your own visiting privileges. The PFV provides the luxury of being able to do some perfectly normal yelling at your spouse.

One of the most common criticisms of the PFV program is that sex is its only real purpose, and that if that were the case there would be something wrong about it. Family unity is the purpose of the program, and all of the benefits for the convict, his family, and ultimately society which that can imply. But if the only reason for these visits were to enable a married couple to have sex together every two months, where is the outrage in that? These men have been convicted of crimes and are duly receiving their punishment of being removed from society and losing most of their freedom and dignity. Must they and their wives also forfeit the most personal sacred aspect of themselves: that is, their marriage? Even the most restrictive religions do not protest the physical unity of a man and a woman within the confines of their marital bonds.

So too, it is not an unreasonable proposition for a married couple to wish to conceive children. Many of these men and their wives would be or already are wonderful parents; making a mistake in part of their lives does not negate the possibility. There are many people out in the world who never commit a punishable crime, but who have atrocious parenting skills, who may be creating, in the youngsters of today, the criminals of tomorrow.

Yet the possibility of achieving conception with such restricted opportunities is a topic of considerable distress to those who are yet childless, but are "trying." When the man is serving a long sentence, starting a family may be a biological impossibility if the couple must wait for his release. The effect, then, of the man's incarceration, can be the particularly cruel and unusual punishment of preventing him and his wife from having any children. This may suspiciously fit some archaic model of prohibiting criminals from procreating, lest there should be some genetically-passed predisposition toward criminal activity.

Predictably enough, the judicial system plods along, much as it has for centuries, postured like the three monkeys with hands over eyes, ears and mouth. People who commit crimes must be punished. So they are locked away out of sight for many years. Most will return to society eventually, yet it is still "full steam ahead" and damn the consequences of our actions, of our society's chosen form of punishment. And when they are released and commit more crimes, let's all play the game and pretend to be shocked at the astonishing recidivism rate. These bad kiddies didn't learn their lesson: Through nothing but their own poor attitudes they returned to us embittered and angry. Guess all we can do is flex our judiciary muscles and return them to where they became bitter and angry, and we'll wait and see if it will work this time.

So in my lifetime and yours there will be prisons, there will be men kept behind bars, and there will be women that they've had to leave behind. It can only become worse before it could ever become better. These men, as all enlightened people are quite aware, are not animals. They are products of our society and symptoms of its failure. Certainly, they have made their own poor choices, but they are not the only ones who suffer.

Out of respect for the privacy and dignity of the individuals involved, I have de-personalized the examples herein. This is not a chronology of my own experiences, although I have shared in many of them. I have had considerable amounts of contact and discussion with many convicts' wives, and I have heard many of the sad tales of their specific struggles.

My mother often told me, "It's better to laugh than to cry." If I shed a tear for every pain of my present situation, I would be unable to continue with my marriage, perhaps even with my life. We hold tightly to what good times we can still have, and treasure our pleasant memories from the past. We pray for a future, and cling tenaciously to the faith that there will be a happy one for us. I need to be strong, and for my marriage to survive, I must weather these times as best I can as I value my marriage highly and love my husband dearly. I accept things as they are now for what they are. To run away from a problem rarely solves it. If I love my husband, should I not stand by him? It is sure as hell not an easy way to run a marriage, but it is my marriage.

I do not ask anyone to bleed for me or others like me. We all have free will which we can exercise to the degree which we choose. However, the price that we are paying is very high, and I wonder if all of these costs are necessary, fair, reasonable or even humane? We are human beings too, each of us with both positive and negative attributes. These are men in jail, but their women live quietly imprisoned within our society. We have always been here, but now numbers are increasing dramatically. We now represent a significant statistical number, but people can so easily ignore what they don't want to see.

We don't want to be forgotten.

Untitled

Diana Hartley · 1988

I've abandoned
pretty fairy tales.

Discarded
three minute miracles
Denied
absolution via the mail.

What I have
may not be much
but it's all mine.

I'm free
standing on
the outside
of the line

Postcard

Diana Hartley · 1986

I received today in the mail a picture
on a card lady white throat gleaming
full lips vampire red pursed open
over the trembling ochre cork waiting
breathless deep green bottle hiding
ruthless phallic intentions inside it
soft black curved brushes of eyelashes
tracing sombre grey rainbows upon
pale skin ivory honey cheekbones
oyster shell carnivorous teeth
flash cruel hard reflections the bowed
carmine head sad and dying rose
plunged like a sacrifice in the heart
empty glass standing silent like an old
forgotten promise spilling refracted colour
the motion of fresh blood that flows
like tears from the torn wounded petals
Is it only my imagination wondering
there is no resemblance between us.

The Window

Evelyn Lau · 1987

Each day she stood for hours in front of the window. It was rectangular, double-plated, fashioned from material that was guaranteed "breakproof." After many years, there wasn't a square inch left that hadn't been defiled with names and pierced hearts, frantic "Gotta get stoneds" and frustrated wiggles flowering over all the other inscriptions.

Her cell was unremarkable. The walls were cement bricks painted white; the ceiling was punched through with barely perecptible holes and painted black. An intercom was fixed in the ceiling; its use was limited to the counsellors' voices calling out reprimands or announcing mealtimes. A mesh slot had been cut into the door, allowing the counsellors to shine flashlights inside at fifteen-minute intervals from lights-out until morning, checking that their captives hadn't strangled themselves with their itchy woolen blankets. Beside a mattress covered in bile-green plastic, a stool and slab huddled unused, they had originally been intended as a desk, but writing materials were forbidden in the cells. A metal sink and toilet squatted in the opposite corner, minus towels and toilet paper. Sometimes she would examine her face in the steel plate above the sink or, clambering onto the stool, her legs. But the plate was dull and obscure.

So she stood at the window, tracing its wounded surface with one finger. Sometimes she leaned against it and cried; it helped pass the cell time. She wondered where the other kids who had been locked inside this cage had gone. To other detention centres and jails? Back home, back to school? It was a strangely intimate experience, caressing their names and messages with her fingertips; she felt as if she knew each one personally. Her own detention hearing had fixed her release date at two weeks from now, but inside the cell there was nothing to mark the passing time.

The window overlooked a parking lot which boasted little activity. It was occupied by police cars and sheriff vans which remained immobile if she watched them, but, like a clock's minute hand, would sneak away the instant she turned aside. On lucky days she would catch sight of a policeman walking by, swinging a brown lunch bag. At night blackness unhinged itself from the sky and clattered down, blotting everything out except the street lamp at the other side of the road. Its silver light washed through the window and onto the floor of the cell. She liked to imagine that it was the glow of the moon.

One day she discovered a spiderweb outside the window, on the bottom right-hand corner. It was in tatters, shuddering at the slightest breath of wind. Once it would have disgusted her, but now she pressed her face against the resisting glass, intent on closer scrutiny. The owner lay shrivelled up on the windowsill, eight legs curled inwards and beginning to crumble. While she stared, her fingernails moved against the window, scratching out a tune for her dead friend.

Dragon's Teeth

J. C. Urquhart · 1989

Some days,
I carry a hundred pounds of fear
through the place where
men wear steel bellies
and the hollow mouths of guns
point hungrily at the floor.

Through the endless corridors
of invisible eyes
through a phalanx of doors
that close
like dragon's teeth behind me.
They wait,
clothed in the green cloth that burns them,
spirits sliding warily beneath.

Morning rises slowly in their eyes.

Some days, words, tossed over shoulders
spring fully grown,
Gleaming like Jason's warriors,
we rise together,
climb aboard the room
sail golden
over dark water.

And I save each breath of grace,
to carry back with infinite effort
through the day
through the steel men
through the gnawing at my heels
through the growling doors

that close shut
and become the walls
behind me.

Razor-wire, Millhaven Penitentiary

Susan Musgrave · 1985

It slices through my heart
the way it surrounds you,
and something the colour of blood
spills out.
In so much blackness the heart
leaps, jumps a beat by the wall and
then goes over.

You've slashed your hands on the wind,
your eyes on a woman's body,
but nothing, not even the stars going out,
has hurt as much as this.

The heart is a gash and
the sky glitters, but all that
high wire coiled and ready to cut
can't keep tenderness out.

The distance between us
is the thickness of blood. Love
jumps away, jumps
out of us.

The Mountains Above Hope

Susan Musgrave · 1989

offer little. Earth and rocks
and black black emptiness
reverse any prayers I might have
had in me. Alone under the bluffs
I still think a life is possible.
Like panic or immediate fear,
I still believe love holds something.

In the Visiting Room at Kent Institution
we just hold on. A guard gulps
ice-water on the other side of the glass.
Your gut is torn and I am naked,
trussed up in the dirt like a wild thing
no man can tame. But you tried.
"I only wanted to love you," I cry.

You cry, too, for the wounds closing over.
It's metaphor, of course, or a bad dream
where we only use love to hurt each other.
It's a risk to feel anything here, inside.
We're both prisoners, guarded. We look at the
mountains but we know we're not going
anywhere. Because there's nowhere

to go. You climb rocks and earth,
out-of-breath into emptiness,
and when you get to the top you have to
start back down.

Your Voice

Lloyd Moffat · 1982

This evening for the first time in
three months
I heard your voice –
But
your voice
was somehow woven into the chains
that kept my arms pinned to
my sides – your voice
was somehow riveting the shackles
that were snarling around my legs
And
as I was pulled through
still another door
your voice
rolled down against my cheek and splashed
against
some silent concrete
that was waiting
for both of us . . .

As John Q. Sees Us

J.E. Telfer · 1985

we talk some
fuck some
suck some
then we talk some more
fuck and suck some more
no plot line
just a beginning, a middle,
and an end
like some low-budget porno flick.

a mis-leading stereo-type at best
a gallows-humour absurdity,
to be sure.

we Love some
Communicate much
Share more
and we repeat it all as many times
as our precious few moments
will allow.

it's not easy to pack
a whole life
into 48 hours
once every two months.

Consequences

J.E. Telfer · 1985

so They locked you away
and Time is passing
while They attempt to achieve
Their oh-so-noble goal:
They try to make of you
an average citizen
and They forget all about little me.

the more They try to socialize you
the less socialized i become
the more They try to civilize you
the less civilized i become.

the more Time passes
the more i hate, the more the anger burns
i become lonelier, colder
the bitterness grows.

and while They're not watching
while They're making you to mould
i've become the dangerous one.

9

VOICING

This final section of "Sentences" concerns the ability to give voice to the process of being imprisoned – from arrest through to survival and points therein. Hence the discussion of the poetic nature of the voice has implications well beyond the literary. Literature in prison cannot be confined merely to academic questions of tradition, form and style. To voice in this context means much more: it involves a statement of self in opposition to the inscriptions which the prison would impose, ready-made. Frank Guiney's "Poetry in Prison" is an excellent summary of the old ballad tradition, of the oral tradition which dominated expression in prisons during the time of the "silent system". Guiney also points to the new challenges which prison writers face in the modern, more liberated prison; there is no longer a captive audience to read between the lines. Prison writing, if it is to gain a larger audience, has to gain it through the quality of its expression. The postcard correspondence between Allen Ginsberg and Rik McWhinney in the B.C. Penitentiary is fascinating in regard to this transition stage between old and new styles of prison writing. The final entry in this section, "Inventive Inventories", is an excerpt from a longer work which I compiled with my students at Kent Maximum, "Through a Panopticon Lightly", prepared for the International Correctional Education Association Conference held in Vancouver, July 8–11, 1990. Following Ginsberg's advice – "don't write poetry, write little fact descriptions of what you see and hear around you with your own senses" – the students wrote descriptions of their cells. From these they chose particular "fact descriptions" to make up an inventory; each writer then chose a set number to arrange in his own order to make a poem which would be his yet also a part of a collective enterprise.

Poetry in Prison

Frank Guiney · 1981

Not too many years ago, when prisons were even grimmer establishments than they are today, when life inside was eighteen hours a day lock-up in a five-by-ten cell with no plumbing, and "recreation" consisted of a twenty minute walk in a single file circle, and "conversation" was talking real low without moving your lips, and "visiting privileges" won you fifteen minutes once a month with a guard at your elbow, and the routine was shaved heads and lockstep and the silent system and bitter black tea and do-your-own-time, and Rule Thirty-Two made laughing a crime, and the "cat" and the paddle were regular reminders that punishment, silence, and solitude were the basic ingredients of repentance and reform, in those days a secret literary art form was already well established and flourishing in our prisons.

Surreptitious in its conceptions and furtive in its lifetime, this bit of underground culture functioned quietly for decades behind grey walls, spreading from cell to cell, from block to block, and from memory to memory by whispered word of mouth. It was a smidgeon of free expression, a part of man that cannot be contained by shackles and bars and concrete; it was a bit of feeling, a scrap of humour, a little release that could not be stifled by the rules and regulations and punishments and deprivations of a caged world.

It was ragged; it was rough; it was cynical; it was ironic. It was funny and it was tragic. It was love and it was hate. It was the "jailhouse ballad" – the poetry of men in prison.

In every sense a truly "inside" culture medium, convict poetry was often bitter and mean, because it was written by men who were often bitter and mean; but surprisingly enough it was just as often sensitive and trenchant and beautiful.

The jailhouse ballad was composed only for other convicts. Seldom did the "square-john", the outsider, encounter a real jailhouse poem, and if he did, he could rarely feel or comprehend its impact, because the experience of the poem could not possibly relate to anything within his frame of reference. Convict irony and convict humour would go over his head and convict sensitivity would fail to penetrate his heart. The joke, the tragedy, the understanding, was ours alone, written between the lines, unspoken, subsurfaced – much in the manner we lived our lives; much like the expressionless faces we showed to our keepers. What outsider could fully understand:

Don't get downhearted, young fellow,
Because you don't get any mail;
The girls soon forget you are living,
They can't use a Daddy in jail.
Oh, they'll cry
And they'll say that they love you
And swear they'll be true to the end –
But the girl that don't bolt
When you're doing the jolt,
Is one-in-a-million, my friend...

Sure, the surface message expressed in those understated anonymous lines is obvious – especially to anyone who has been a loser in the love game – but only another prisoner could fully appreciate the gut-wrenching agony and despair alluded to by the unknown writer. Whoever he was, he knew exactly how to probe at a most sensitive and vulnerable place in a prisoner's heart, with precisely the right mixture of irony, humour, and poignancy.

To anyone who has "done a jolt", that little stanza conjures the whole painful story – a story of hope and good intentions and resolutions and love and longing and broken promises; of clinging desperately to a bit of solidity in a sea of loneliness; of predicating your whole life on faith in another. It's a story of rose-coloured glasses and starry eyes shining through wire mesh screen, eyes alight with the often mistaken optimism that love conquers all. And it's the grinding frustration, the soul-killing story of the frailty of the human condition when the inexorable, debilitating CRUSH of the time tests its slender underpinnings. It's a story of bitterness and tears and insanity; of slashed wrists and hanging bodies; of broken dreams and broken men; of a shrunken world of helplessness and despair...three paces long and an arm's-stretch wide.

It's an unwritten story directed to other prisoners in other five-by-tens in other restless nights.

That was the old prison poetry – for prisoners only.

How many square-johns ever heard of "The Ballad of Morphine Bill", or "The Dope Fiends' Convention", or "Three Way May"? Or the multitude of verses scratched on the walls of holding jails across the country?

These were the real jailhouse ballads of yesterday, composed behind bars, committed to memory, and repeated in the sweatshops and work gangs for the appreciative ears of contemporaries . . . when the "bull" wasn't looking. If the ballads were good, they endured, were passed on, and they eventually spread from coast to coast, handed down through generations of prisoners.

But the poems remained within the bounds of the prison culture and the "rounder element".

Once in a while an exceptional talent would attempt to "bust out", to tell it the way it is, to try to communicate in the language of the real world; or occasionally, as in England, the rare genius of an Oscar Wilde might be thrust into the mysterious, distorted half-life of prison existence, taste of its bitterness, and then try to convey the stultifying horror of the caged and the damned to those who cannot know.

But even then, given the genius of Wilde, I wonder how many people of his time could reach deep enough into *The Ballad of Reading Gaol* to smell the disinfectant and the fear, to hear the echo of clanking steel and the eerie moans of tortured sleep, to feel the real hunger-ache in a man looking up from the dankness of a concrete pit – for "that little patch of blue that prisoners call the sky."

We knew. Because that kind of prison was part of our lives. And you can believe it; there are still Reading Gaols in this country.

Things are changing, of course, ever so slowly. Penitentiaries and jails are mostly old unwieldy monsters that seldom lend themselves easily to enlightenment and new concepts, but the prison secret, the isolated inviolate mystery of yesterday, has been breached, and there are ever widening leaks in the concrete curtain. Prison poetry has changed with the times. Part of the reason is likely because pencils, pens and paper are no longer scarce bits of contraband, and the old oral tradition is no longer necessary to the preservation and dissemination of the poems. As a result, few prison poems are written in the style and form of the original jailhouse ballads. Prisoners today explore a much wider range of expression in their poetry.

Perhaps a more significant factor in this change is the increased contact that today's prisoners maintain with the outside world. Communication is still severely limited in many prisons, of course, but even the most backward maximum security penitentiary today allows visiting and writing privileges that would have boggled the minds of old-timers. With this limited medium of expression and communication on the increase, jailhouse poetry began to take on a new look back in the 1950s.

Prisoners who cared about such things came to realize that the feelings and ideas that they expressed on paper would now be read by people unfamiliar with the prison ethic, and that these feelings and ideas might even be more important to some outsiders.

So prisoners still write poetry; but its scope has widened, taken on new tones. Just as prisons are not as mysterious as they were thirty years ago – or even ten years ago – neither is prison poetry. And it may be that outsiders understand more and listen a bit closer and even care a little.

But the poetry of the prisons still retains a certain uniqueness, and is an art form in its own right. The form and styles are not as distinctive and easily recognizable as the old jailhouse ballads, but most of them contain a flavour and spirit by which they can be identified – at least by other prisoners.

Yesterday's jailhouse ballads are fast disappearing. No one memorizes them now. Maybe somewhere, some place, someone has compiled a collection of them for posterity; or perhaps some old-lag or lifer has a few tucked away in the dusty obsolescence of his memory – but for the most part they are probably lost forever, buried under layers of paint in city lock-ups or laid to rest in unmarked graves in the shadow of the Wall.

And if the ghosts of yesterday's legion of unknown, unsung jailhouse poets are peering over my shoulder tonight, I can only ask their forgiveness for a woeful ineptness in trying to do what they would have done much differently.

I'm sure they would understand; because there is something about a prison cell that awakens in almost everyone a craving for expression, a need to communicate (if only with one's self); an urge to spill out the pinpointed, polarized emotion of the moment . . . in one way or another.

Give any prisoner a stub of pencil, a scrap of paper, and an empty, swelling ache in his chest, and something truly genuine and beautiful could someday emanate from that five-by-ten he lives in. There's steel and concrete in there; and a toilet. There's some bloody history and a multitude of sad memories; there are three walls that "steal the light and give nothing back in return"; but there is also a very human being in there,with a heart, with a soul – and with at least a few of the saving qualities of mankind.

Some of us still recall a piece of free verse (no pun intended) which circulated through the British Columbia Penitentiary about twenty years ago.

Its origin and its author are unknown to this writer but its message, certainly, will be forever contemporary. Maybe that particular jailhouse poet summed up what we are all trying to say, in one way or another:

See that guy over there?
That's me.
If you don't believe me
Go and ask him.
But don't be surprised
If he says he's you.

Untitled

J.S. · 1954

This poem won the 1954 Transition *poetry contest. The judges, unidentified outside arbiters, cited its "humour" appeal.*

I am just a fellow inmate,
Not so smart and not so muggish,
But I like to write in rhyme
nothing classic, nothing sluggish.

I've been told that our *Transition*
offers prize to poet or writer
Who produces words of wisdom
Lines of poetry, profound or lighter.

Although I'm not a hoggish person
Full of larceny or greed,
I still have a keen ambition
To maintain myself in "weed."

So I offer to *Transition*
Lines of poetry, panegyric,
Hoping you'll see fit to publish
Some of these attempts at lyric.

If by chance I please your reader
With my rhymes both trite and terse
Let me know and I'll deliver
Heaps and loads and scads of verse.

If I fail to make impression
If my verse should be provoking,
I'll just crawl into my corner
Forced at last to give up smoking.

Merry Christmas Mother

D.B. · 1954

This poem won second place and was cited for the "sentiment" expressed.

My thoughts, here, this time of year
Echo scenes of home and you;
Restless thoughts that bring a tear
Remembering debts of love past due,
Yet, Mother, I feel you near;

Close in spirit, close in thought,
Hoping, praying for your son;
Recalling the paths you sought,
In vain, to set his feet upon.
So, results, Mother, I got,
Through years, months, sun to sun.
Much as I deservedly ought
All those years have passed, are done,
Selfishly and dearly bought.

May I, this way, Mother mine,
Opened as my eyes are now,
Tell you that your heart's design
Has brought me to realize how
Empty was that life. Thus I'm
Remembering, with true greeting now

Telegram From Solitary

Rik McWhinney · 1975

Back in the same cold cell
Where possibility closes the final door &
the great void remains. . . .

Stop 24 hour blinding light, dirt, spit &
blood on walls
Stop brutal beatings & broken hand knuckles
scraped raw in protest
Stop depressing suicides
What reason forced monastic existence
Stop cruel & usual
Screams of anger penetrate
Stop solitary confinement
The vortex of this rage & shock
of consciousness.
[Stop.]

The Penthouse

Memories haunt this prison cell
Images that weave a vicious spell
An empty gaze upon the walls
finally broken as the shadow falls

Dying sunlight trapped in spring
enhance the echoes of desperate loneliness
Where once in time & for the rhyme
Will always ring.

The McWhinney-Ginsberg Correspondence

Rik McWhinney

July 27, 1979

Dear Rik McW,

No time to correspond. I asked City Lights to send you a pack of books of mine.

If you get a chance, to correct yr. corny poetry style, read the regular factual no-bullshit poetry of W.C. Williams (William Carlos Williams) if you can find any in anthologies. He is straight forward. No pretty roses & corny thorns, images that have been re-used "like razor-blades" till they're dulled. "No ideas but in things." That is, don't write poetry, write little fact descriptions of what you see & hear around you with your own senses, with simple real knife & fork & spoon & napkin & cup words, forget 5 & 10 Store Beauty, forget "Beauty" but write about real details of a fence or bed or wall or moon or hand or daydream or car exhaust noise or cough, if you want to communicate to others.

Allen Ginsberg

Aug. 27, 1979

RIK MCWHINNEY
Solitary Confinement
B.C. Penitentiary

Dear Rik McW.

I can't keep correspondence, travelling.

Yes, Whitman for spirit (breath) expressed in *minute details,* lots of little red wheelbarrows & red chickens in Whitman, and a drop of perspiration falling off the mustache of a prisoner on chow line-up.

You can only write *for real* about details you observe with your 6 senses (sight, sound, taste, touch, smell, mind a combo of the other 5), you'll only make loud noises about anything more abstract, but when I see a spoon thru *your* eyes, I see thru your eyes. Like you see thru W.C.W. or W.W. or A.G. Ground your mind in minute particulars, "take care of the little ones".

Allen Ginsberg

August 10th, 1989

Hello Peter [Murphy],

Greetings from the gulag. I apologize for not responding to your earlier missive, but having just completed 16 years of a life bit, my mind is geared towards an upcoming parole hearing. I am enclosing the 2 cards to which you refer. Much of my Ginsberg correspondence has been lost or destroyed through prison transfers & riots. Anyway I hope the cards serve your purpose well. I no longer write poetry, in fact I never did, except for my earlier bastardized style of expression. I enjoy putting down my thoughts & observations on paper, but lack the discipline of structure. I am presently studying the comparison of Ginsberg & Whitman. Particularly "Howl" & "Out of the Cradle Endlessly Rocking." I am also pursuing the work of Algernon Swinburne, but the library here is inadequate. Will you please help me acquire a particular poem of his, title "Laus Veneris" . . .

Keep Punching Champ

Rik

Inventive Inventories

Readers and Writers Cooperative, Kent Maximum · 1990

I. Venting

Only time will tell.
For the ducts contain dust,
blown in by the hot
dry summer air

A vent, high in the wall,
seems to serve no purpose
other than to rearrange
the dust . . .

It seems to be everywhere
It appears mysteriously
almost
magically.

The air duct
is my worst enemy.

II. Remaindered

The cell is, as I stated, temporary.
Cardboard boxes stuffed under the bottom bunk.
Metal lockers with combination locks
To lock up our valuables.

Imprisonment is unchangeable.
Two steel bunks fastened to one wall.
Screws crudely embedded into plaster.
Only people are changeable.

I read the walls, swept the floor, used the toilet.
There's not a lot of things to do.
It's count time.
Eleven o'clock and the day is over.

The cell holds what it should.
Nothing.

III. Circulation

The air duct is my worst enemy
Dust seems to be every place
It appears mysteriously, almost magically
The porcelain of the sink & toilet gleam with virginity

I read the walls
Sweep the floor
Use the toilet
There is only so much I can do

It's count time
My door is closed for inventory
Only muffled sounds seep through
These walls now suck the years out

Forcing the awkward, mechanical door
I look both ways, as taught when a child

PART II

PAROLES

10

THE PEN: A SELECTION OF PHOTOGRAPHS

Donald Lawrence
Historical images compiled by Tony Martin

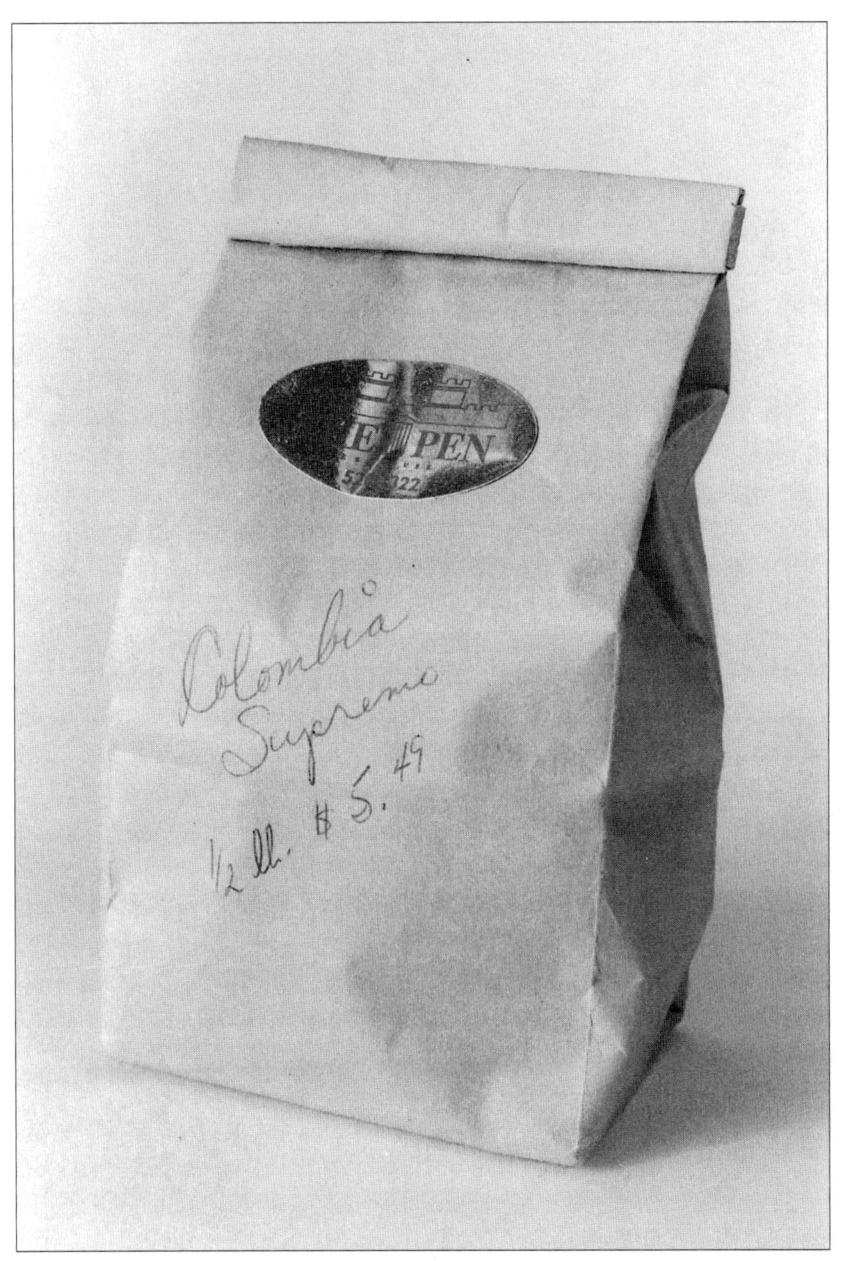
Colombia
Supremo
1/2 lb. $5.49

Demolishing Wall.
Columbia Street,
February 20th, 1932
B.C.P.

103
A-G
CLOSED
Cell Block
Hair Design
MARILYN MONROE
MasterCard
MasterCard
Monday Closed to Ferme
Tuesday 9:30 5:30
Wednesday 9:30 5:30
Thursday 9:30 9:00
Friday 9:30 9:00
Saturday 9:00 5:00
Sunday Closed Ferme
VISA
A-G BACK TO SCHOOL
PUSH
CAQTI

Desserts Check our display
BEER
TAX EXTRA

New Westminster

Alexander Forbes · 1992

river boats press
broken images into water

past counterfeited houses, little
more than sheds – unreliable witnesses to
roads long delivered to lilacs and wallflowers

past bankrupt streets falling into railyards where
warehouses roofed in tin, are paroled to grass –

past a penitentiary astonished, open mouthed, empty:
a prison with a history of unguarded moments

across a channel of unsettled reflections
until the city is seduced by distance –
a fugitive acquaintance denied

11

BILL MINER: PAPER TRAILS

Bill Miner, the most famous outlaw in Canadian history, was an American. Miner was notorious for his train robberies in British Columbia (see the fine Canadian film, *Grey Fox*, starring Richard Farnsworth). His escape from the B.C. Pen in 1907 was even more successful in making him a *cause célèbre*. Tom Elton's sequence of poems on Bill Miner – written while Elton was in prison at Ferndale Institution, a stone's throw from where Miner staged the first Canadian train robbery at Mission Junction – recreates the romantic aura of the outlaw Miner, but also suggests through the prism of time a sense of critical distance for assessing our fascination with the outlaw as hero. The second part of this chapter juxtaposes excerpts from the official penitentiary file on Miner's escape. The Penitentiary Service's attempts to place the blame for Miner's escape on prison guard Alex McNeil (who was fired) and on Deputy Warden Bourke (who was forced to retire on a pension) are riddled with historical ironies in light of the argument recently put forth by Mark Dugan and John Boessenecker (1992) that "they were but scapegoats offered up to protect those who evidently engineered Miner's escape: the Canadian Pacific Railway and the office of Inspectors of Penitentiaries Office." In their view, the Grey Fox played his hole card, the whereabouts of the Australian securities taken in the Mission Junction robbery, in order to negotiate his escape. An impartial investigation of Miner's escape was never made.

The Trails of Billy Miner

Tom Elton · 1988

DINNER AT THE KEG

Would you care for dessert?
I'll try the Bill Miner pie.

ON A PHOTO OF BILL

Jets of steam released
cause the whistle to scream, shrilly,
signalling the arrival
as the train pulls in to berth
at the Sapperton station.

A crowd of curious onlookers gather
to catch a glimpse of
the outlaw in a checkered coat.

Miner steps from the train
into the crowd's hush of expectation.
Eighteen links at a time, he shuffles
to take his place in the wagon
that will carry him to the B.C. Pen.

A *Columbian* reporter gets his shot
as the Fox pauses. In that caught flash
Miner is once more, an old man
wearing chains and a frown
on his way to life.

POSSIBILITIES

Riding the Fraser Valley grubline
thinking of the possibilities, the Grey Fox
with not much coin left to jingle.
Each next meal is a farmer's smoke rising
in the distance, a white curl
against the bluegreen mountains.

More miles and the old bones aching more.
He finds there's not much to do in Mission
except stagger his drinks
and listen to farmers and loggers complain
about mosquitoes and the dry spell.
Bill tells tales about the men he's met
on the trail, their outlaw exploits
legendary in the North.

Comparisons between the countries are made:
stages are rarely robbed in Canada,
most people travel by C.P. rail, perfectly safe,
as proved by the mountains of gold
mined, and then shipped out
from Bralorne and the Kootenay region.

Too many meals missed. Too many
cold nights spent on the ground. Old bones
getting older. Canada, the virgin land, ripe
for someone with a one track mind.

What time does the train get in? he asks,
thinking of the possibilities.

OUTFOXED

Noted for its cunning, the fox
will climb and follow a fence-rail,
criss-cross the countryside,
or enter burrows the pack can't get into
to throw off its scent, making sure
all pursuit is lost before
it heads home to its den.

Bells toll now over the black river.
A ladder is found leaning
against the prison's south-west wall,
suggesting a breach. A further check reveals
a hole dug under the fence,
four of the prisoners missing.

Work parties escorted in are locked up,
releasing guards from boring duties
to join the excitement of the hunt.
They search the ravine beside the prison
and all surrounding areas, but

the wily Fox eludes
the braying pack again.

BREAKFAST NEAR MISSION

Four days on foot.
Miner follows the thin forest paths
into the Fraser Valley.
The prison falls behind him
like a bad memory, like
the banks of the river he criss-crosses.

He threads himself between trees,
rocks, bushes as he moves.
He touches each, as if each touch gives
him a cloak of invisibility.

His hunger is a growing hand
squeezing his stomach, demanding food
more substantial than
the river's rising mist
in the grey dawn streak.

A farmer's smoke is a risk
taken near Mission. He eats "enough food
to satisfy three men," before moving
deeper into the valley where
friends in Chilliwack lend a hand
for further flight, and safety
in the lands of the Similkameen.

POLLS AND GAMES

Who? What? When? Where? Why?
These are the basic questions asked
by a curious *Province* reporter
on a wet, downtown Vancouver street
four days after Miner's escape.

Four ticks for; one tick against.
The random survey clearly concludes
a tell-tale affinity between
the man-in-common and the outlaw
who robs trains and banks
growing prosperous at the people's expense.

After dinners of roast beef, potatoes,
carrots and gravy, Bill Miner is served
like a dessert, his latest exploit
a mouthful to be savoured.

He's no stranger to people he's never met.
He is more like a distant friend or,
like an uncle who comes and goes
suddenly, every five years or so.
"He isn't a bad man, really, just a man
who's had some bad breaks and now
the Police won't leave him alone."

In back yards and streets of towns
little boys point sticks at one another,
argue bitterly about who gets to play
the outlaw or the sheriff,
the outlaw being the favourite role.

"You're under arrest."
"I'm Bill Miner. You can't keep me."

From the Bill Miner File, BC Penitentiary, 1907–09

Confidential
Office of Commissioner of Dominion Police
Ottawa September 3rd, 1907

Geo. W. Dawson Esq.,
Inspector of Penitentiaries
New Westminster, B.C.

My dear Dawson: –

I understand from the Minister that you are out there conducting an enquiry into the escape of the notorious "Bill" Miner and I have heard something recently which may turn out of consequence. From a very reliable source I learn that the Acting-Warden *was warned* about Miner's probable escape some days before it actually occurred and am further told that he and those with him are supposed to have made their escape through a hole under the fence, whilst good judges with whom I have been in communication feel confident that they made their escape *through the gate* just close to where the hold is and the party who was on guard that day in the Tower is alleged to have had the keys of the gate and is suspected of complicity. It is further stated that Miner's *hair and beard* had been allowed to grow to a considerable length before the escape. I give you this for what it is worth.

Very truly yours,

A.R. Sherwood
Commissioner of Police

The Penitentiary
New Westminster, BC
Sept. 16th 1907

[Inspector of Penitentiaries] Stewart,

I enclose herewith file 305/07, and minutes of evidence taken by me respecting the escape of Convicts Edwards (Bill Miner), McCluskey, Clark and Woods on 8th August 1907. I think it is evident that Guard McNeill was negligent, but there is no evidence at all to indicate that he directly or indirectly, passively or otherwise, wilfully assisted the convicts to escape. I have heard of nothing that points to connivance on his part.

He failed to patrol his beat anything like as often as he ought to have done. He says himself he patrolled the walk only once every half hour (page 28). During the afternoon of the escape, Instructor Doyle saw McNeill "probably every ten minutes" but did not see him once on the walk (page 34). Guard Walsh saw McNeill many times that afternoon, but did not see him patrol his walk once (page 42). He appeared to be talking to someone near his stand (page 43). Convict Thos F. Young, now at large on ticket of leave, says McNeill was talking to him off and on all that afternoon (page 24). I accept Convict Young's evidence with some reserve. Instructor George Mackenzie says Convict Campbell told him McNeill was held in conversation by Convict Young at the time of the escape and for some time before (page 44). If McNeill had patrolled his walk even once every ten minutes, I think the escape would have been prevented. Clearly his negligence gave the convicts their opportunity.

McNeill is not alone to blame. He did not exaggerate when enumerating his duties as guard on Stand 3 (page 26). He had more to do than watch the west fence. It is a fact that the gate to the piggery was left all day unlocked (pages 23 and 26).

The brick yard was not operated last year. Since it was operated last, the north and west fences were erected (see plans). A stand, No 12, was provided at the north west angle. A guard in this stand would have a clear view of the north and west fences, and of all those parts of the brick yard not visible from Stand 3.

A guard ought to have been posted on Stand 12. Mr. Bourke says he had not a guard to spare (page 12). He had Guard Walsh, but he posted him on the ground to oversee the men at the Kiln, where he could not see the west fence (page 142). Mr. Bourke thought if McNeill patrolled his walk he would see all parts of the yard. He thought every fifteen or twenty minutes often enough to patrol the walk but admits that if the hole the convicts escaped through had been dug in advance the convicts could have got away within fifteen minutes (page 8). Clearly a guard ought to have been posted on Stand 12. Mr. Bourke thought the yard safe with McNeill practically alone to guard it (page 22).

Mr. Bourke was warned on 1st July by the Revd A.D.E. Owen not to give Miner too much liberty (page 1). Nevertheless he transferred him from the shoe shop to the brick yard, because he thought he was breaking down and he wished to give him a change (page 14) and his feet were blistered and swollen (page 22). The surgeon did not know that his feet were sore (page 6). The hospital overseer had not seen him for sore feet (page 7). Mr. Bourke felt sorry for Miner who is getting old and sick. He treated him as well as he could (page 1).

Mr. Bourke in his letter of August 23rd (pages 1, 2 and 3 of this letter) says he suggested to the Warden certain alterations in the stands and fences. They were not made. He was in charge in June when I was there. He said nothing to me respecting these alterations because he was afraid the Warden would be offended, and he did not want to antagonize him (pages 11 and 18).

Miner's hair was not long when he escaped. His moustache was clipped. It appeared about as it would be with three weeks' growth after shaving (page 50).

The escape was discovered within five minutes after it occurred (pages 32, 36 and 37). No time was lost in sounding the alarm. The prison was closed promptly and the officers were sent out in pursuit with as little delay as possible. The reports of the officers who were sent out are submitted.

Mr Bourke says he is convinced that the escapes were planned for his downfall (see his letter of Sept. 6, page 8, attached to minutes of evidence). Need I say there is not a shadow of evidence to support his belief. I think without doubt the convicts were aided by confederates outside. I think the hole was dug from the outside. I couldn't account for the total disappearance of all four convicts if they were not skilfully aided when they got out (see convict Campbell's statement page 57). Warden Whyte is very ill. I am forbidden to speak to him respecting any matter that might agitate him. I cannot examine him respecting the visit of McIntyre, Bullick and another man, with whom Miner is said to have been unaccompanied by any officer (pages 49 and 51).

Convict Campbell, I think, shows how the convicts exchanged letters with friends outside (page 56).

I enclose Guard McNeill's resignation. I recommend that it be accepted.

I enclose also a letter from Mr. Bourke in which he intimates that he desires to retire from the service "if his retiring allowance can be arranged satisfactorily."

I recommend that he be retired and granted such allowance as may be lawful.

Yours faithfully,

G.W. Dawson

S. [Mr. Stewart]
October 15/07.

Dear Mr. Dawson, –

Re escape of Miner et al.

There are two or three points in this case in which definite instructions could not be given in a letter to the Warden and which the Minister desires you to look into and set right.

(1) From the evidence it appears that the piggery gate was left open during the day with little or no supervision. It seems absurd to make heavy expenditure for stockade and then leave a point of egress unguarded. If it is necessary and safe that a convict should work outside the stockade, the Minister thinks that it should at least be so arranged that an officer would in passing through the gate as he goes out lock the gate until such hour as the convict is required to re-enter. This is a matter that you have no doubt given attention to, but, in case the papers should be called for at any time, it is well that your action should be on record.

(2) It appears that there is a ladder attached to a stand near Cumberland Ave. by which the convicts scaled the outer stockade. The Minister desires you to consider whether it would not be safer to have the ladders brought in, except when required for actual use. As I understood the matter, this stand is unused for weeks and even months and it seems unnecessary that facilities of this kind should remain during such periods. No doubt the convicts would have escaped if the ladder had not been there, but it seems bad policy to allow a custom that will facilitate escape.

(3) The Minister is anxious to have more information with reference to the mysterious visit of McIntyre, Bullock, and the unknown, who were apparently allowed to interview the convict without supervision eight or nine months ago. It is not likely that McIntyre will give any information, but, perhaps if you can obtain the address of Bullock, it will be possible to have on file his statement of what their business was and also whether they were allowed to interview the convict without official supervision. The matter was quite fully referred to in instructor McKenzie's evidence. If you desire the file, I will forward it.

Yours sincerely,

[unsigned; Mr. Stewart]

Warden's Office, New Westminster, B.C.
Oct 22nd 1907

Dear Mr. Stewart,

I have your letter of the 15th instant regarding (1) the piggery gate (2) The ladders used in ascending to the guard stands, and (3) the visit of McIntyre, Bullock and another, to convict Miner.

(1) The day after my arrival here I ordered that the piggery gate be locked and kept locked except when the convict in charge of the piggery was being passed through by the hall guard. As soon as it could be made, I had a spring bolt fitted on the gate that is opposite the prison entrance and so arranged that the guard on stand No 2 can open or lock the gate at will. The convict who is attending the pigs wheels the kitchen refuse

through this gate and down a new path to the piggery. The piggery is in the ravine 100 feet below stand No 3. A convict running from the piggery towards the river would be in plain view of the guard on stand No 2. The piggery is in as safe a place as it can be without being in the inner yard where it would be a menace to the health of the prison. One short time man is in charge. There is always the chance that he might attempt to escape, and the guards on the stands Nos. 2 and 3 know it, and keep watch. A twelve foot board fence surrounds the ravine in which the piggery is situated.

(2) A twelve foot fence surrounds the farm field and the ravine. At different points there are stands, seven or eight in number. One is used when the farm gang happens to be working near where it is placed. When no work is being done in the fields the stands, of course, are unoccupied. Ladders are used to reach them. One is secured by chain and lock to the fence below each stand. When an officer has occasion to mount the stand, he unlocks the ladder, mounts by it and pulls the ladder up after him. Farm work may call the gang from one field to another, or from one part of a field to another part, perhaps several times a day. The guard to keep them under supervision would have to move to the stand commanding the part of the field to which the gang had been removed. It might be risky for him to carry his ladder from one stand to another. The practice is for the gang to fall in at a proper distance from the occupied stand, the officer then descends, locks up his ladder, and marches the men to the part requiring their labour, here he halts them, unlocks the ladder at the stand he is to occupy, mounts and pulls the ladder up and then the gang goes to work. Of course the ladders will be brought in and locked up *if it is so ordered.* If this is done, it will be necessary to keep the gang at the prison until the guard is on his stand, and probably it will be necessary for an extra officer to accompany the instructor, to see that the gang reaches the field in safety. This will be awkward, and there will be the risk to run every time the guard finds it necessary to change his stand. He will have to carry his ladder when marching his men to the new field of labour. He ought not have anything in his hands that might interfere with his instant use of his rifle if necessary. On the whole I think the present practice is as free from risk as another. The axe that broke the lock securing the ladder Miner used would soon have opened a way through the one inch boards of which all

the fences here are constructed. The fences are a trifling obstacle to a man at large. At best they give the guard on the stand a chance to hold a gang, working near enough to fear his rifle. The stands of which I speak are the "farm stands". Nos. 0, 1, 2, 3, 4, and 12, our inner yards stands, have enclosed bases in which are stairs leading to the stands.

(3) If I can obtain Mr. Bullock's address I shall ask him to inform me regarding the visit referred to in Mackenzie's evidence. Yours faithfully

G.W. Dawson

S. [Stewart]
October 29/07

Dear Mr. Dawson, –

The Minister was much pleased with your supplementary report of the 22nd. inst. with reference to the action you have taken to secure the piggery gate.

As regards the ladders attached to the different guard stands, it is, of course, not practicable to have them carried back and forth every day during the season that the outer guard stands are in use. From the correspondence it appeared to us at this distance that a number of the outer guard stands were used only during the farming season and that between seasons it would be safer if the ladders were brought in. That is a matter however which you can judge on the spot to better advantage.

Yours sincerely,

Inspector Stewart

Remarkable Escapade

The New Westminster Columbian · *August 7, 1903*

Sometime ago it was noted that a patient at the hospital for the insane had escaped. The patient was Mr. Vogel, a gentleman having, it was said, considerable property at Rossland, and whose mental trouble takes the form of belief that people are seeking to take his property away from him. Vogel escaped once before, secured work and behaved sanely enough. However, he told his fellow workmen about the alleged designs of his relatives on his property and his story reached the ears of the asylum atuthorities, who located him, and brought him home again.

When Vogel got away the other day he was evidently well aware that a strict search would be made, and he rose to the occasion. He somehow procured a ladder and made his way to the Penitentiary. Reaching one of the walls, Vogel put up his ladder, climbed up where he lay snug until the hue and cry quieted down a bit. Then he left Warden Whyte's domain in the same easy manner as he had entered it, and departed, nobody knows where. He left the ladder behind to tell the story.

12

THE VIA DOLOROSA OF VLADIMIR MEIER

Compiled, translated and edited by Tom McGauley and Jack McIntosh, 1992

Vladimir Meier, Russian poet, arrived in Canada after involvement in the early Soviet revolutionary period and sought some kind of temporary refuge in this country among the Doukhobors. Meier came into the midst of the ostensibly pacifist Doukhobors at the moment of their deepest turmoil. In October of 1924 their divine leader had died in what was taken by most to be an assassination, and the corporate body of the Doukhobors, the Christian Community of Universal Brotherhood, was entering into the mid-stages of a highly fractious bankruptcy. These were some among the myriad factors which led to a protracted struggle of the Doukhobors which found an external focus in a long confrontation with the Canadian government. One of the results of this spiritual combat was that hundreds of Freedomites were made inmates of the Canadian prison system.

Meier was sentenced to six months' hard labour for his part in a demonstration which the authorities had broken up while Meier was attempting to mediate between the Sons of Freedom Doukhobors (who saw themselves as "liberators of all humanity ... [and] every animal enslaved by man") and the provincial police. He was transported from Nelson to Oakalla Prison farm. After a few months confinement he crawled out of his cell, scaled a guard tower and shouted that he wished to be returned to Russia. To face death at the hands of the Bolsheviks, he argued, was better than one "from the smiling bullets of the English". A few days later, on the 2nd of January, 1930, he died in the provincial psychiatric hospital.

200 Douks arrested at Nelson Saturday

Grand Forks Gazette · *September 27, 1929*

RIOT ACT READ BY MAGISTRATE – LEADERS OF RUSSIAN GROUP RESISTED BUT WERE TAKEN BY POLICE

NELSON, Sept. 21 – Acting under instructions from the Attorney-General's department following a report made yesterday by an official from Victoria as to sanitary condition of Doukhobors camp, just beyond the city limits, the provincial police shortly before noon notified the 200 hundred or more encamped Sons of Freedom to move.

The final result was the arrest of the entire group by about thirty officers, including city police and specials, after the reading of the Riot act by John Cartmel, government agent and provincial magistrate, had failed to secure their obedience.

LEADERS OFFERED RESISTANCE

A physical clash occurred when Maloff and other leaders, whom the police first took in hand, resisted arrest and the officers were at first thrown back. The police, however, concentrated on these men, and the body of adherents on seeing them disappear into a big car, made no further resistance.

Under nominal guards, the Doukhobors, chanting as usual, were marched to the provincial jail. The Doukhobors, whose claim that they had no home was nullified yesterday by their being offered Porto Rico, one of the lumber camps of the Christian Community of Universal Brotherhood, are technically vagrants. They are also rioters, and have also interfered with the police in discharge of their duties.

While Inspector Forbes Cruikshank directed the operation, Mayor R. D. Barnes was present, the city authorities lending both moral and physical support. The first group arrested were booked as resisting arrest, and the balance on a charge of vagrancy.

Report on Doukhobors in B.C.

J. H. McMullin, Superintendent, B.C. Provincial Police · November 4, 1929

"... That an element of Bolshevism, originating with the Independent Doukhobors, has entered into the affairs of the Sons of Freedom, is becoming plainer as events develop. This is first noticeable when in May 1928, on the resumption of hostility to sending the children to school, one Anatole FAMILIART or Anatole FOMIN, not a Doukhobor, was found very active agitating among the malcontents comprised for the most part of Sons of Freedom who have been banished from the Community by young Peter Verigin for not living up to the conditions. Familart, up to January 1928, had been living in California. He came to Grand Forks about that time and spent all his time agitating and spreading Bolshevik propaganda. In B.C. the centre of Bolshevik activities seems to be Thrums, while in Saskatchewan, where there are even larger numbers, the centre is at Kamsack. Man named Victor KAFT or KAFDARATZE, Boris SOKATOFF and Andrew KAZAKOFF are said to be the leaders there. During recent disturbances at Nelson an agitator named Pete MALOFF arrived in a car from U.S. and actively addressed the disaffected Doukhobors. Another man, Vladimir MEIER, a non-Doukhobor who claims to have been a Czarist officer, was equally prominent during the disturbances. Ordinarily this man – his name suggests a Jewish origin – and those like him would scarcely sympathize with the Doukhobor peasantry and it is a fair conclusion to believe that the presence of Meier was actuated by some ulterior motive. Both Maloff and Meier were arrested for obstructing a Peace Officer and are now serving a sentence of six months' imprisonment at Oakalla ..."

Vladimir Ivanovich Meier: Obituary

Peter Maloff · 1930
Translated by Jack McIntosh

During the past decade Russians have scattered over the whole world. War, revolution, and especially the civil war have undermined and shattered the last energies of many children of Russia. Many have had to lay their bones down in far lands without waiting for smiles of consolation and joy.

One of these was V.I. Meier, who died January 2, 1930 in the psychiatric hospital to which he had been transferred five days earlier from Oakalla prison, near Vancouver, British Columbia. A native of Kursk Province, 38 years old, a former student at Moscow University, he had a dual personality, one entirely Russian: at times quiet and calm as a deep lake on a hot summer day, but at other times tempestuous as a raging ocean during a storm. He had a great heart, broad as the Russian steppes, with a soul deeper than Mother Volga.

He came to us in 1924 from Bulgaria – broken down and exhausted in soul and body. At our very first encounter he cried: "O British mountains, may you relieve my distress; if not, then crush me like a worm!"

Volodya told us about many terrible and painful experiences from the time of the civil war. It was obvious that these trials had deeply affected his whole life.

"How can I be calm," he would say, "When I took part in fratricide and saw innocent people crucified and other horrors which can never be justified. I served with the Reds – it was terrible. I went over to the Whites – it was twice as bad. I saw Greens and Blues – followers of Petlyura, Makhno, and so on and so on – and there was horror and shame everywhere."

"Yes, Tolstoy was right," he would often reiterate, "If Russia had heeded his voice, she would have seen neither reds, no whites, nor other masters. She would have preserved all her sons and there would not have been the ugliness which now reigns and may continue for a long time."

They arrested Volodya along with eight of us Sons of Freedom Doukhobors as agitators and for resisting the authorities – entirely false accusations. They found us guilty based on false evidence. Four policemen who were nowhere near us gave evidence, and we were sentenced to six months in jail. This had a powerful effect on Volodya: from the first day of confinement his stomach gave him trouble – he could not eat any of the prison food. For two months the doctor paid no attention while Volodya continually begged and implored them to let him go to the hospital or to give him milk and fruit. We also petitioned on his behalf, but to no avail. One Sunday Volodya came to my cell and said: "A little bird flew to my little window – she is calling for me to go there, out into infinity; I feel that the end of my earthly existence is near." The next day, to everyone's amazement, he crawled through the bars (the bars are six inches apart) at the height of the fifth storey and wormed his way, at great danger to his life, onto an old guard tower attached to the prison wall, and began to shout from the top, demanding that he and all of us be immediately released. "If you don't want to let everybody go, then release me right away or send me back to Russia. I am not afraid of the Bolsheviks. Let them shoot me. I would rather die at the hand of the Bolsheviks than from the smiling bullets of the English." They began to beg him to climb down, but he went on declaring that he would come down only if they granted his request. They gave a promise that they would let him go, and he came down. Then they locked him up and said they would take him to the hospital.

Soon they did take him away, but we later found out that they did not take him to the hospital, but instead to the insane asylum, where within a few days he died of causes unknown to us. The head of this "psychiatric" hospital later informed us that Volodya was extremely exhausted, could not take food, and had died of "exhaustion brought about by his mental illness." It was not until fifteen days later that we learned of his death, and that from sources other than the authorities, who would tell us nothing and disavowed even what they knew about his death.

Over the five years of my acquaintance with Volodya, I came to love him deeply. With his great heart, this person with every fibre of his soul strove to help others and to pour at least a droplet of joy into the hearts of suffering people. I shall long remember the bright minutes of my life when he openly shared with me his profound experiences. He had a lot to tell me, a son of the Canadian prairies and mountains, yet of kindred spirit with the peaks of the Caucasus. He related many marvellous and secret things about that land which had nurtured him and Tolstoy and

Dostoevsky and many other brilliant names which perhaps could never be found anywhere else in the world.

Rest in peace, dear friend and brother. You have honourably finished your life's path. And if there were secrets you did not disclose to us, it is not for us to judge you – we all have them.

Oakalla Prison, British Columbia
January 20, 1930

PS: When I am released, I shall try to send you Volodya's poems, which express his spiritual state and his hopes.

The Cranes

Vladimir Meier
Translated and adapted by Jack McIntosh
and Tom McGauley

Flocked cranes swim single file
Some hide, my eyes chase others flying
yearning to overtake their height

Mustn't scare them, they're hiding
I can hear only a little clucking
One sighs so deeply – why?
They've flown off! Does it matter?

With bursting spring light I would high, high fly there
and forgetting this our bitter life
sing the cranes' song

While below me fields newly green widely spread beyond.
See dawn-tinged storm clouds
rising over horizon's edge

May spring warmth, life's joy
bud and grow in my heart
then may that precious first light
illuminate my winged path.

RUSS [USSR] II

Vladimir Meier
Translated and adapted by Jack McIntosh
and Tom McGauley

To My Favorite Poet, Aleksey Tolstoy:
"To everyone, everyone, everyone . . ." – Aelita

Can Russia be broken apart
are window and door behind barbed wire?
No, the road to her has not been cut.
We need to love her now

She is Russia, Rus' – alive –
ever and always alone
around barrows of fresh green,
where by-gone's rattle of spinning-wheel
steadily hums through the years

Leafed oak groves rustle
and smell of grasses comes in rivulets
grey wolf's mythic howling
jasmine's colour sad to the tender heart

Don't forget the meadows
And teetering churchyard crosses
And geese honking through spring nights
Did you know Russia in its simplicity?
Be healed with the country babkas.

And then go lie down
in rye's full blooming sea
And understand that all the old sayings live
Their all is not yet fully disclosed

As you pass through droves and flocks
barefoot on fresh grass, love them
Divine your fortune in any beetle
and never kill anybody

In evening's deepest dusk
you'll understand even Red Moscow
as her sons caught up in hurricanes
spread dawn's tidings

So that the whole world would
"live and have mercy"
My Land gave itself
and more beautiful yet
it arose from the grave
And went home,
into the fields.

13

THE HOSTAGE: THE MARY STEINHAUSER CASE

The death of Mary Steinhauser, a young classification officer, during a hostage-taking incident spearheaded by Andy Bruce in 1975 was the most infamous incident in the history of the B.C. Penitentiary. The *Vancouver Sun* report on the day of the fatal shooting captures some of the dramatic sequence of the events and the responses of those present. The most effective recountings of the hostage-taking took place not in an inquest or a judicial enquiry in camera, but on the stage. The Steinhauser incident led to plays by Christian Bruyere and Sharon Pollock. The final scenes of these plays make for an interesting series of dramatic contrasts in terms of the Mary Steinhauser – Andy Bruce relationship and their versions of the actual shootings. In both plays, the prisoners' fears of solitary isolation are developed as key motivational factors in the hostage-taking. Andy Bruce was to testify in the fall of 1975 with others in a lawsuit against the Crown concerning the nature of punishment in the SCU (Special Correction Unit). It was ruled that such imprisonment was "cruel and unusual".

Woman hostage slain by bullet

The Vancouver Sun · *June 11, 1975*

A woman hostage was killed by a bullet through the heart as the siege in the B.C. Penitentiary ended in a blaze of gunfire early today.

One of her captors was critically wounded but 14 of her fellow hostages were freed safely from the penitentiary vault where they had been held for 41 hours by three desperate inmates.

Mary Steinhauser, 32, had spent most of the 41 hours with an inmate's knife at her throat, but she was killed by bullets fired when a tactical squad stormed the vault area as the hostages battled the inmates.

New Westminster Coroner Doug Jack reported at noon today that Miss Steinhauser had suffered two bullet wounds.

And although police chief Rod Keary told a press conference she had apparently been stabbed, Jack said no knife wounds were apparent on her body.

The coroner said an autopsy showed that one bullet went through her shoulder and the fatal bullet penetrated the same shoulder, continued on through her heart and left lung, and lodged on her right side beneath her eighth and ninth ribs.

Jack said he had not determined the calibre of the bullet but "it was a fairly substantial-looking slug."

Miss Steinhauser was pronounced dead on arrival at Royal Columbian Hospital.

Inmate Andrew Bruce, 26, was admitted to the same hospital in critical condition after being shot during the frantic moments that abruptly ended the inmates' bid for freedom at about 1 A.M.

After surgery on facial and abdominal injuries, Bruce's condition was given as serious. He is expected to survive.

The other two inmates, Claire Wilson, 26, and Dwight Lucas, 20, were taken to New Westminster city jail. Lucas suffered superficial head injuries but did not need medical attention.

The trio, all serving life terms for murder or attempted murder, had held the 15 hostages in the vault since 8 A.M. Monday, threatening to kill them unless the government gave them a helicopter and safe passage out of the country.

Solicitor-General Warren Allmand said in Toronto today that the government had made no firm decision to agree to the prisoners' demands. However, he said one country approached by the government had agreed to accept the trio, incarcerate them on arrival, and return them to Canada as soon as possible.

Later, Allmand told the Commons he has recommended that the cabinet order an inquiry, headed by people outside the penitentiary service, into the incident.

Shock and confusion followed the outbreak that brought the long ordeal at the penitentiary to its tragic conclusion.

Police Chief Keary said it began with a confrontation between some of the hostages and convict Wilson in the storage vault.

He said Bruce and Lucas, in the office outside the vault where Miss Steinhauser was being held, were alerted by the confrontation.

"It was at this time that Mary Steinhauser was apparently stabbed," he said.

Keary said the tactical team then moved in and "shots were fired."

Chief Keary emphasized he has not yet gathered all information on the incident and he said this won't be complete until charges are laid later this afternoon.

He said police inspector Ed Cadenhead is heading up a team of investigators at the prison.

Asked if he could provide any further details on Miss Steinhauser's death, Keary replied: "I can't tell you that until the autopsy is completed later today by New Westminster coroner Doug Jack".

Asked why he said she was "apparently stabbed," he said, "We hear that from people there."

Asked if he knew whether or not she was shot, "no, other than the report I heard on the radio."

Keary said that to his knowledge only Bruce was shot.

He said the tactical squad which was drawn from a prison team of 30 to 40 special officers entered the room about 12:45 A.M.

He said eight shots were fired but he said he did not know from what kind of weapon.

Keary also said he did not know who gave the command to enter the room and start firing although the tactical squad is under the over-all command of prison director Dragan Cernetic.

Keary said the incident was touched off when one or more of the hostages attacked inmate Wilson. Following that, inmate Lucas was apparently attacked by the hostages and clubbed on the head.

Keary said it is not clear yet which inmate, if any, stabbed Mary Steinhauser.

Reporters at the scene were told by others, including an ambulance operator, that Miss Steinhauser had been shot.

Broadcaster Gary Bannerman, one of the team of five intermediaries through whom negotiations were carried on with the inmates, reported she was stabbed and possibly shot as well.

But a doctor listening to Bannerman's radio report in Royal Columbian was overheard telling a colleague, "That's funny. I didn't see any stab wounds."

The sound of muffled pops in the still night signalled the start of the tragedy about 1 A.M.

Guards raced from their turrets atop the prison walls and sighted their rifles at the classification building where the hostages were in the storage vault.

Inside the prison shouts spilled out into the night from excited voices.

"That had to be shots," said a reporter as press, radio and television reporters and photographers ran for the front gate area of the prison.

Penitentiary Director Cernetic stopped them short.

"Nobody moves from that point. That's an order," shouted Cernetic, pointing to the sidewalk about 15 feet from the gate.

"Get the front gate open," Cernetic barked, and an ambulance that seemed to come from nowhere entered the penitentiary.

A prison guard wearing a riot helmet emerged from a side door.

In a matter of minutes one and then a second ambulance, the second had been on standby inside the prison, raced out the front gate for the hospital.

In the first ambulance reporters could see someone massaging frantically the person inside.

Cernetic appeared again and warned reporters they could not leave the prison grounds until further notice. Some reporters said they saw a man walk from one part of the prison to another with knives covered in blood.

Ambulances arrived and lined up outside the front gate.

A penitentiary vehicle loaded with guards and, as it turned out, two of the inmates, left the front gate and headed to the New Westminster jail.

The time was 1:15 A.M.

Fifteen minutes later Jim Murphy, regional director of the Federal Penitentiary Service, pleaded with reporters at a press conference not to release information until relatives of the hostages had been notified.

Asked privately if the ordeal was over, he said: "It's all over."

But the wait continued for details.

When he finally returned, he announced the death of hostage Mary Steinhauser and "at least two inmates have been injured."

He said the prison staff did not trigger the incident. They had strict instructions to take no action unless violence occurred first, he said.

Penitentiary officials refused to release a list of hostages this morning.

They said it would have to be approved by Regional Penitentiaries Director Jim Murphy, but that no action would be taken on it until a meeting later in the day.

Murphy and B.C. Pen director Dragan Cernetic both went to their homes to sleep after the exhausting siege ended early today.

However, *The Vancouver Sun* talked to relatives of two of the hostages, and identified them as classification officer William Taylor and counsellor Vic Kuzyk, 54.

They also went home to sleep, and had little to say about the experience.

A niece of Taylor said he phoned home to say he was out and safe, and arrived home about 3:30 A.M.

"He was very tired and worn out, and said he had been instructed to treat the whole matter as confidential," the niece said.

He went straight to bed and would probably sleep for most of the day.

Kuzyk's mother told *The Sun* that her son and the other hostages had all their personal possessions "thrown away" by their captors soon after the ordeal began.

"My son said that they took their wallets, rings, money, everything," she said.

She said her son had arrived home at 4605 Alpha in Burnaby about 3:15 A.M. and was still sleeping with the aid of sedatives.

She said he was not injured in any way, just tired and very relieved the ordeal is over.

Mrs. Kuzyk described the 41-hour siege as a "tense, fearful time with little sleep" for her family.

She said her son's wife and two children spent most of the time switching from one newscast to another hoping to hear details of the hostages' fate.

Mrs. Kuzyk said she had cut short a visit to Edmonton and returned last night to be with the family.

Many of the hostages were in a state of shock. Bannerman reported that the prison chaplain, conducting a brief service for them in a waiting area, broke down during the service.

At 2 A.M. Canadian Forces personnel who had set up a command post at Vancouver International Airport were told to "stand down."

The command post had been established in the event that a deal was made to fly the convicts out of the country. Emergency communications equipment had been set up and a search and rescue helicopter was standing by to pick up them and the hostages from the penitentiary.

Assistant B.C. penitentiary director J.P. Bulltitude said all visiting privileges at the prison remained cancelled, but the prisoners would receive their usual exercises today.

He reported that the mood inside the prison today was quiet.

The other prisoners were "not sympathetic with this at all," Bulltitude said.

He said New Westminster police had sealed off the vault area to conduct their investigation.

Chief Keary said he was satisfied that the prison staff and director had done everything possible to avoid the loss of life.

Asked if there was any forewarning of the hostages' plan to jump the inmates, Keary replied: "No, I don't think the officials of the prison knew."

Keary said Wilson and Lucas would be kept under police guard at the New Westminster city jail pending charges later today, while Bruce was under guard at Royal Columbian Hospital.

He would not say which charges were being contemplated, but did say they would cover all the incidents beginning Monday morning.

Asked if he was concerned about security at the penitentiary, Keary replied: "The penitentiary is a concern to me as it is in my area of police administration."

"In a place like that with 500 inmates, some of them dangerous, you never know what is going to happen."

Prison officials said an investigation will be held into the system which allowed the prisoners to plan their bid for freedom.

Walls, Scene 17

Christian Bruyere · 1978

In Walls, *Christian Bruyere depicts Mary Steinhauser as an idealist who had "the guts and compassion" to challenge the prison system, "to help the inmates." The play has a two part chronology which Bruyere "felt necessary to process the information prior to the hostage-taking as well as the forty-one hour ordeal." Scenes 1, 5, 8, 13, and 17 are a fictional recreation of the events which took place at the B.C. Penitentiary on June 9–11, 1975. Scene 2 begins nine months earlier and the other scenes develop in chronological order from Scene 2. Andy Bruce is Danny Baker, Dwight Lucas is Luke Douglas and Claire Wilson is Curt Willis – the hostage-takers, and the Steinhauser character retains her own name, Mary. Other characters in the final scene are Kevin, a classification officer; Jim, a security guard who has become a classification officer; Hadley, a medic; and Hiller, a security guard.*

The classification office is lit. MARY *is asleep on the chesterfield.* DANNY *is taking another fix.* LUKE *quivers nervously beside him.*

LUKE: Help me.

He puts his hand on DANNY*'s arm. He gags, almost vomits.* DANNY *holds him.*

DANNY: Hang on in there, brother.

LUKE *relaxes.*

LUKE: Brother?

DANNY: Yeah, brother, I need you.

LUKE: You say that like you mean it.

DANNY: I do mean it.

LUKE: Really?

DANNY: You know I do.

LUKE: Wherever we go, huh, let's do it as a team, all right?

DANNY: Sure, man, you and me.

DANNY notices LUKE's hand on his arm. He goes to the tape recorder and plays Jimi Hendrix' "The Wind Cries Mary." MARY awakens.

MARY: Give me a break, will you?

Having woken MARY, he rejects the tape. LUKE glances at MARY.

DANNY: Hey, man, why don't you go guard the vault?

LUKE drags a chair to the vault doorway. He sits on the chair. First, he becomes nauseous, then he nods off. DANNY is worried. He moves MARY's legs to allow himself some room on the chesterfield.

JIM moves slowly towards the vault door. KEVIN finds the tripod in the vault and grips it tightly. Both men have a shield of clothing wrapped around their arms. They plan their attack.

MARY: I just had the strangest dream.

DANNY: Tell me about it.

MARY: I was a little girl back in the Kootenays and the lake was rising; it just kept rising and rising. It flooded the fields and the garden and the house and the barn. And then I heard a squeal. It was Petunia, my pet pig.

DANNY: Your pet pig?

MARY: The runt. I bottle-fed her myself. She couldn't swim, so I jumped in after her. My dad told me I should have let her drown because I couldn't take her to the city with me. So I ran away with her. We went deep into the woods, deeper and deeper. I got cold and hungry so I built a fire. I was outrageously hungry, I mean, it was unreal. My stomach growled till I became faint. Then I stared at Petunia and she pushed her little snout into my hand. She used to do that when she wanted a little love. But I picked up this sharp stick. She tried to get away, but I jabbed her and kept jabbing her until . . . until she was dead.

DANNY: Take it easy, will ya?

He rubs her legs to comfort her.

MARY: [*Almost hysterical*] Then I cooked her. And as I was taking the first bite, I saw all the people I knew around me, my friends and neighbours, and they just laughed and laughed. They wouldn't stop laughing.

DANNY takes her in his arms.

DANNY: Mary, I love you.

His lips go to hers. KEVIN *and* JIM *lay back down.* DANNY *glances towards* LUKE. *He attempts to awaken him. He is out cold.* DANNY *nervously paces back and forth.*

MARY: Two down.

DANNY: And two to go.

He takes CURT*'s knife and hands it to her.*

MARY: No, Danny.

DANNY: Take it.

MARY: No.

She stands and walks towards the window.

DANNY: They've abandoned you. You served their purpose and now they're going to let you die.

MARY: What are you talking about?

DANNY: You're the guinea pig. They set you up to challenge their system, but they cheated you. They made you run a maze that had no exit.

MARY: No, Danny, you're the guinea pig. You'll prove them right if you hurt anybody in there.

Their eyes lock.

MARY: If you really love me you'll put away that knife.

There is a pause. He stares at her and places his knife in his belt. He puts his arms around her. She returns the caress.

DANNY: All right, lady, you got the faith. Prove me wrong.

KEVIN *motions to* JIM *in the vault. They make their move now,* KEVIN *comes forward, the tripod gripped above his head. He smashes it down on* LUKE*'s head, once, twice, three times.*

JIM goes for his knife. LUKE will not surrender it. DANNY turns, puts down the camera and grabs his knife. JIM runs back into the vault. He yanks KEVIN back with him.

JIM: Watch out for Baker.

He closes the vault door. DANNY and LUKE struggle with the door, but cannot open it. HADLEY appears in the entrance way. He yells back along the hallway and enters the classification office.

HADLEY: Hit it. Hit it.

LUKE: Curt. Curt. They closed the fuckin' door.

LIZ and CURT wake up. MARY is in shock. The hostages scream for help. DANNY grabs MARY and takes her roughly to the vault door.

DANNY: That's it, you son-of-bitches, you've done it now. You've fuckin' killed her.

KEVIN: Go ahead. We don't care.

HADLEY: Take it easy, you guys. Open the door.

Three GUARDS rush in to the classification office in stockinged feet. They are carrying .38's. HILLER is one of them. He takes aim at DANNY. DANNY swirls around, with MARY as his shield, his knife above her head. LUKE runs for cover behind the chesterfield.

DANNY: We're going home, Mary.

HADLEY: More demerol? Don't shoot.

GUARD: Freeze. Drop the knife, Baker.

Seven shots are fired rapidly. The first two seem to hit LUKE. He is down. DANNY is hit. His mouth explodes with blood. He and MARY are brought to their knees.

MARY: Don't shoot him, he won't . . .

They are both hit twice. They fall to the floor. MARY is dead. HILLER hops over their bodies and goes to the vault.

HILLER: Open up. It's all over.

The vault door opens. HILLER *takes aim at* CURT. LIZ *shields him.*

LIZ: Don't hurt him.

HILLER *yanks her to her feet and pulls* CURT *out by the hair. They enter the classification office.* LIZ *sees the bodies.*

LIZ: Is she dead? [*To* DANNY] You bastard. You killed her.

An eighth shot is fired from one of the GUARD*'s .38's. It barely misses the second* GUARD.

GUARD: You goddamn idiot!

HILLER: Get 'em out of here.

He collects the .38's from the two GUARDS. *They take away* LUKE, *who has not been hit, and* CURT, *from the vault. The hostages follow.* LIZ *stays behind.*

LUKE: [*Struggling with the* GUARD] He didn't kill her, they did.

DANNY *points to* HILLER. LIZ *is stunned.*

LIZ: He wouldn't have hurt me.

HADLEY *escorts her out.*

LIZ: [*struggling against him*] Get your hands off me.

HILLER *stands over* DANNY. DANNY *is scooping the blood away from* MARY*'s body.* HILLER *aims his .38 at him.* DANNY *stares back at him defiantly. The second* GUARD *re-enters with a stretcher.* HILLER*'s arm relaxes. They all freeze.*

The lights fade slowly. DANNY*'s solitary cell is lit. Only the cell light remains on.*

Final Scenes: *One Tiger to a Hill*

Sharon Pollock · 1981

Sharon Pollock's play also covers many of the well-documented issues of concern at the B.C. Pen: the abuses of solitary confinement, the resentment against any progressive "do-gooders" (especially a woman in a male world), the jockeying and squabbling for power between the prison administration and the guards' union. But she frames her play very differently in order to emphasize its impact on the audience as a very real social and moral fable. In this regard, the character of Everett Chalmers, "a corporation lawyer, early thirties," who is brought in to help with the negotiations, is crucial. Chalmers speaks to the audience in the opening and closing speeches of the play. In the opening scenes, Chalmers does not "acknowledge the presence of the other characters" and is in a sense the "narrator," introducing the play proper of which he was a part with the words, "It happened like this." Pollock distances her characters from the actual B.C. Pen hostage-taking incident through the choice of names for the principals: Dede (Deed) Walker plays the Mary character, Tommy Paul, a Métis, takes the Andy Bruce role. Most importantly, Pollock does not present these two figures as lovers; indeed, it is the rejection of Paul's romantic interests by Dede that is the vital factor in the final scene, a reading which goes against the grain of most hearsay about their relationship. Other characters in this final scene are Frank Soholuk, a rehabilitation officer, late twenties; Gillie MacDermott, hostage-taker, in his twenties; Carl Hanzuk, a guard, mid-twenties. Any reader of the play will also enjoy the portrait of Claire Culhane as Lena Benz, "A social activist, old leftist, about sixty." Of special note: both plays use musical excerpts from the BC Pen Symphony, *composed by J. Douglass Dodd.*

WALKER: Tommy –

PAUL: This is it, Deed.

WALKER: We gotta talk! We gotta talk now!

PAUL: We're not talkin', we're doin'!

WALKER: What're we doin'?

PAUL: Gettin' outa here!

WALKER: Then what?

PAUL: Be together, you and me!

WALKER: That's not gonna happen, can't you understand that!

PAUL: What're you gettin' at, say it!

WALKER: I –

SOHOLUK: What's the matter, Deed, you run outa words?

WALKER: Tommy, I –

SOHOLUK: You wanna know something funny, Tommy? Out on the street they're all talkin' about the chance of your cuttin' our throats – well the jokes on you, man, cause she took you out months ago. Sure, you're dead, man, and she's been workin' the strings. You're her model prisoner, don't you know, prime example of the Walker rehabilitation method.

PAUL: What are you sayin'?

SOHOLUK: People like her don't love people like you.

PAUL: What's he sayin'?

SOHOLUK: Go on, Deed, we're all waitin' to hear it.

GILLIE: [*Shoves Stocker out of the way, grabs Soholuk, knife at the throat*] Shaddup!!

PAUL: Deed?

WALKER: What?

PAUL: Do you love me?

Pause.

WALKER: [*Softly.*] No.

PAUL: What?

WALKER: No . . . I . . . do love you Tommy, but not in the way that you think.

PAUL: You love me as what.

WALKER: I love you as . . . as a person who's been . . . fucked up, and screwed around but – that's as far as it goes.

PAUL: [*Screams*] Noooooo!! [*He backhands Walker across the face. She falls to the floor, having spun around with the force of his blow so that she is face down. Paul kneels beside her, grabs her hair, yanks her head back, her neck exposed. His knife goes to her throat. He freezes. Pause.*] . . . I love you. [*He releases her. She falls forward. Gillie is frightened. Pause. Then Chalmers gently takes Paul's arm, helps him up. Walker remains on the floor.*]

GILLIE: Tommy?

PAUL: . . . It's . . . it's O.K. . . . it's O.K., Gillie . . . it's O.K. . . . it's alright . . . I mean . . . I want . . . And you . . . [*A gesture towards Chalmers not complete.*] . . . and . . . ah . . . hey . . . you know . . . it's better this way.

WALKER: Tommy I –

PAUL: Don't you say nothin'! There's nothin' to say! . . . it's O.K. Gillie . . . hey . . . you know . . . I feel light, light as a bird. If I were a bird I wouldn't need wings, I'd just float over the wall.

WALKER: Do you really feel that?

PAUL: Sure. I was worried. For you, I was worried. Now there's just Gillie and me and I . . . I . . . You . . . got a pretty face, Deed, you got a kind face.

WALKER: I'll go out with you just the same, just for show.

She holds out her hand. Paul pauses before he takes it, then brusquely, in a very quick movement he grabs her hand, yanks her to her feet, drops her hand quickly.

PAUL: I'm gettin' itchy feet! Time to go! Time to go, Gillie, you hear that, time to go, Chalmers!

Hanzuk is standing in the tier corridor just upstage of the stairs. He stands parallel to the wall, his left shoulder down stage, his head turned to glance over that shoulder. Although we cannot see it, his right hand holds the gun.

McGowen enters unobtrusively. He is merely a shadow at the end of the tier corridor. We might see the glow of his cigarette.

Wallace sits at his desk with a drink in his hand.

All in a soft freeze.

CHALMERS: We got . . . a couple of minutes.

PAUL: Coupla minutes, coupla minutes, coupla . . . hey . . . you know McIver's cafe, the all-nighter cafe 'bout four blocks east a your office?

CHALMERS: On the strip.

PAUL: That's the one . . . I was standin' down there – a while back – and this big black caddy pulls up, I told you this, Gillie. And this big black hooker hops out, man, she's sailin', people are partin' like the Red Sea, she comes up to the all-nighter cafe, someone opens the door, she never breaks step past the booths to the back where Jerry McIver is standin'. She sails up, sticks an ice pick in his gut, turns round, back past the booths, someone opens the door, hell, it mighta been me, the car's at the curb, she steps in – and she's gone. . . . Can . . . you . . . understand that?

CHALMERS: Understand what?

PAUL: I'm thinkin' . . . you can die . . . and all it is is a moment. . . . You're gonna walk out with us, eh?

CHALMERS: Yeah.

PAUL: You don't have to do that.

CHALMERS: I want to.

PAUL: I suppose . . . you got a wife and kids and a house.

CHALMERS: Two kids.

PAUL: I know there's a life out there different from mine.

CHALMERS: Tommy –

PAUL: I got choices, man!

CHALMERS: Yes.

PAUL: Well? . . . Come on, Gillie, let's go!

The electronic sound begins faintly and grows in volume during the following scene. There are no footsteps, gates, or rattling of keys, only a whining hum.

PAUL: Let's go! Let's go! Check the hall. [*Gillies does so.*] Come on! [*To Soholuk and Stocker.*]

SOHOLUK: Look –

PAUL: [*Shoves him.*] You with Gillie, Deed with me.

SOHOLUK: [*To Chalmers.*] Who's out there, eh?

GILLIE: Real quiet, nobody there.

PAUL: [*Shoving Stocker into a chair.*] Sit down and stay!

SOHOLUK: [*Back to Paul.*] Tommy you –

PAUL: Shaddup! [*Gillie grabs Soholuk, knife at the throat.*] Hold him close and tight, Gillie, Keep a good space between us, O.K.

GILLIE: Gotcha.

PAUL: O.K.

The electronic sound is just discernible.

PAUL: Let's do it.

Chalmers steps out of the outer office. He is followed by Paul with Deed. Gillie waits a bit before following them. He is just into the corridor, Paul with Walker about centre stage, when Paul stops.

PAUL: Wait a minute.

CHALMERS: What is it?

PAUL: Nothin' . . . Deed? . . . Hey Gillie? [*He doesn't turn to look at Gillie. Walker is still held close and tight in front of him. Chalmers has turned to look back at Paul.*]

GILLIE: Yeah?

PAUL: I changed my mind . . . I want you to let Frank come up here, and you bring out Stocker.

The electronic sound is clearly heard and increasing in volume.

GILLIE: Eh?

PAUL: It's O.K. We're gonna take Stocker and Frank with us. I want Deed goin' out with Chalmers . . . no sweat, man . . . Frank, you come up here when I let Deed go.

GILLIE: [*Is confused.*] I let him go now?

PAUL: [*Turns Walker round to look at her.*] Go on Deed.

Walker moves towards Chalmers. Paul turns back to look for Frank. Hanzuk takes a step to the top of the stairs, gun aimed down the corridor.

GILLIE: Now?

Electronic sound loud. Hanzuk fires once. Paul turns, sees him, screams, and runs towards him.

WALKER: [*Screams.*] Nooooo! Nooooo!

Hanzuk fires a second shot hitting Paul who falls. Gillie has released Soholuk and crouches like a child, his hands over his ears. Soholuk has darted towards the outer office. They are in a soft freeze. Walker, on seeing Paul hit, runs from Chalmers towards Paul. As she reaches him she looks up at Hanzuk to see him recovering from the recoil of the second shot, and aiming at her.

WALKER: Noooo!

Hanzuk fires. Walker falls close to Paul. The electronic sound is fading and gone. Chalmers stands staring down at Paul and Walker. Silence. Chalmers speaks to the audience.

CHALMERS: I remember I stood there . . . looking down . . . and I thought . . . if Paul doesn't move the blood from his jaw will run into her hair . . . but he didn't move and neither did she. . . . What were the lies? . . . Is everything lies? . . . tomorrow . . . I said . . . I will have breakfast . . . drop . . . the kids off at school . . . on Friday . . . I'll go to the Y . . . [*He weeps.*]

BLACKOUT

14

THE CASE OF THOMAS SHAND

Tom Shand's court statement gives the prisoner's side of a hostage-taking incident at the B.C. Penitentiary in the "stormy 70s", post-Mary Steinhauser period. Tom Elton's prose and poetry use a very different type of language to offer an "in memoriam" for his friend who died under strange circumstances.

Statement of Thomas Mason Shand

Tom Shand · 1977

The following is a statement read to the court at New Westminster, B.C. on April 25th, 1977, by Thomas Mason Shand, prior to his sentencing for taking part in a hostage-taking incident at the British Columbia Penitentiary. The incident was part of a much larger disturbance/riot in the penitentiary during which one wing was taken over by the prisoners.

Mr. Shand: Your Honour, I should like to read a statement that I prepared and I should hope that the court would understand that I am not referring to this courtroom or to any individual in this courtroom, that I am talking (when I talk) of courts across Canada. These are my own personal feelings and I hope that they won't have any effect on the sentencing of these other individuals. I'm saying something that I think has to be said. I would hate to see someone else persecuted for what I said. I have made the statement myself, I have had no help in the preparation. It's my statement. If it's all right with Your Honour, I should like to go ahead with it.

The Court: Surely.

Mr. Shand: I have pleaded guilty to all these charges after spending 7 months in solitary confinement. I have come to realize the futility of preparing a proper defence against the charges laid. If I thought I stood even a slight marginal change of receiving a fair and impartial trial, I would take this case to high court. But as other inmates before me have found out all they can expect and receive from the courts of this land is ridicule and degradation.

Here I stand before this court chained like some wild beast, with a heavy guard around me to emphasize my alleged dangerousness. One can only wonder for whose benefit all this show of security is for. I can assure the court it certainly doesn't benefit us, the accused. I should like to ask you, sir, how can any judge or jury ever be expected to believe any defence we may put forward with this ominous cloud cast over us. We stand before this court depicted as animals not capable of functioning in any other way than the way you have portrayed us here. How can anyone ever give us the benefit of the doubt when the courts have gone to such a great extent to take any doubt away from us that there may have been?

I am going to try to explain to the court how all of this came about even though I know you have made up your minds as to what happened and what kind of people we are. Truth no longer enters into this case: if it did, others would be standing along side of us. They would not be inmates, they would be penitentiary officials charged with inciting to riot and conspiracy. But as we have seen by other court actions this will never happen because the sacred white horse must be protected at all costs. I should like now to try and explain to the court why we had to resort to taking hostages.

As most of you know by now the riot was simmering for the better part of three days before it became full scale. In these 3 days prior to the major riot not one thing was done by the administration to curb the impending riot or to alleviate the tensions that then existed. The only party trying to get things back to an even keel was the inmate committee who were met with opposition and open hostility by the administration at every turn. On the subsequent day of the riot we were working in the kitchen while a full scale riot was in process in the East Wing. It had been going full blast for some 2 hours. I still to this day do not understand why we were permitted to be out of our cells when such an explosive situation existed. One can only conclude that the administration wanted the ensuing events to take place. We were made to understand that custody was in the process of getting ready to rush the East Wing with tear gas and clubs to subdue the rioters. We knew there was also the possibility of great loss of life to our brothers because many of them were quite prepared to die for their cause.

There was no doubt in our minds as to the seriousness of the situation. Things had deteriorated too far to hope for a peaceful settlement, so when we were asked to take hostages, we did because it was the only thing left to do. We then took 8 and 9 hostages, thereby creating a Mexican standoff. I should like to state here and now that at no time during the 27 hours ______ was held or the 81 hours imposed on ______ was either one subjected to ridicule, physical abuse, or idle threats. They were treated as best as the situation allowed and every precaution was taken to ensure their welfare and safety. Another myth I should like to try to dispel is that contrary to popular belief by the prison administration and the committee investigating prison violence that the inmates did in fact everything in their power to stop the riot and hostage taking long before they were ever conceived. All their pleas and requests fell on deaf ears from the Solicitor General's Office right on down the line.

It is my opinion that had the committee acted in any other way than they did there most certainly would have been some loss of life and they would have been derelict in their functions and duties as elected members for the inmate population. There has been much ado made of the hostage takers and the rioters and virtually nothing is said of the hostage makers and the riot creators, which can only be compared to cattle being blamed for stampeding and the cause of the stampede being left unchecked so that there may be other stampedes.

The Solicitor General's component of the Public Service Alliance association has such overwhelming power that they are able to create a disturbance or a hostage taking in any maximum security penitentiary in Canada at any time they so desire. They can and have done this many times in the past and will continue to do so in the future unless drastic measures are taken to curb their awesome power. They are able to create incidents to justify higher pay and tighter security measures. What they are in fact doing is asking for a 24 hour a day lockup for all prisoners in maximum security institutions, thereby eliminating all the dangers to themselves. And at the same time asking for a high risk pay when there is no longer a risk factor involved. All this is done at the expense of the inmates who are manipulated into situations and the public who must bear the brunt of this form of blackmail where the hidden message is "give us what we want, or we will set the animals loose."

It is fantastic when you consider that just 17 years ago it cost the Canadian taxpayers $27 million to run the prison system which today costs 10 times that amount. With what result? Is the crime rate down? No! Are related training programs improved? No! As a matter of fact they have disappeared for the greater part in our maximum security institutions, leaving a large part of the population idle. The only winners in today's prisons are the guards who get higher pay and the outside contractors who build more slaughter houses. The losers are you the public who get nothing in return for your investment and inmates who will one day be coming back to your society to thank you for all that you have done for them. They will probably be so thankful that the next time you send them back for a trade or psychiatric treatment they will probably try to kill you to prevent you from doing so.

It is my honest opinion that each and every one of you knows the injustices that are committed against the inmates in your prisons. I include the more than 100 deaths which occurred in the last five years in the Federal prisons of which more than 80 have been attributed to suicide. But you know better than I do, nothing has been done to seek out the real reasons for these deaths or the perpetrators who committed them. Yet you sit back and wonder why there is no longer respect for the laws of the courts and the people who make the laws of Canada are more criminal than the people they send off to prison. You have powers and authority collectively to do something about the deplorable conditions which exist in our prison system. You have created a mammoth monster which you no longer have control over.

All I am able to say in my defence is that had there been a more peaceful way to bring about the cessation of hostility we would have tried that way first. When inmates in a prison can no longer negotiate peacefully to have their complaints and grievances heard by Ottawa and the public, then they will do it violently because they know you understand violence. Sometimes we are forced into situations which we do not necessarily want to participate in but the circumstances surrounding the situation give us little or no choice but to participate.

Thank you sir.

The Court: Thank you Mr. Shand.

The Mediator

Tom Elton · 1989

Thomas Mason Shand never figured he'd be "disappeared." But he was, and not in Chile or Argentina but in beautiful British Columbia, Canada.

Born in backwater Ontario in the '40s, Tommy reached national notoriety in a Calgary alley during the winter of '65. A police beating that went wrong became a Capital Murder charge and subsequent death sentence for him. After a number of years on death row that sentence was commuted to life.

Tommy was presence from the first day he walked into a federal penitentiary. He never entered a room; he occupied it. It was this that made him so visible. And it was because of this visibility that guards and prisoners alike sought his help and advice. Quite naturally, he became a mediator. And in that role he excelled.

During a three day prisoners' strike at Saskatchewan's Prince Albert Penitentiary, it was Tommy's mediation that set things right. It was also, however, his mediation that earned him a quick "kidnap" transfer to the west coast's B.C. Penitentiary. There he reassumed the role left behind at Prince Albert. However, for a time, those skills were little used. And then there was a riot.

July 1976. Death by gunfire was threatened and expected. The prisoners' committee was being either ignored or threatened as well. Tommy was called to mediate. He and others ended up taking hostages in the prison's kitchen area. A standoff had been achieved. No gunfire took place. No one was killed. The riot burned itself out. He and the others were charged and taken to court.

Like most other prisoners Tommy worked his way down through the institutional security levels to a day parole and half-way house. He attended university, worked, fell in love, and rediscovered a rapidly changing world. For the most part things were fine. Life was looking up.

There was a darkness, however. Ever since the Calgary murder, every Christmas, Tommy would get an unsigned card from that city. Within that envelope would be a hotel reservation, the date of the reservation corresponding to the anniversary of the date of the Calgary murder. He never knew who reserved the room or sent the card, but suspected it wasn't a friend. Nor did he figure it to be any of his friends that tried to run him down one night while he was ten-speeding home. Just who these people were remains unanswered.

In the summer of '84, Tommy was "disappeared". Months later his body was discovered in a secluded part of forest by a hiker. A Coroner's Court ruled it suicide; cause of death, hanging. It proved to be a sentence he was never able to escape.

To Tom Shand

Tom Elton · 1989

The men next door are making love,
squeaking bedsprings loud through the plywood walls.
Hoarse whispers awaken me:
"Move it. Move. Tighten up."

I think of you and me, Tom,
running laps around the Pen's dirt yard,
or playing scrabble for pushups
to kill the too long days and evenings,
ignoring the twenty year difference between us.
We were indifferent to the salvos fired
by a roaring public censure.

Next door they breathe in gasps.
One moans with pain and pleasure,
the other groans
(unconcerned about waking me or what I might think.)
The wall between our cells shakes
with each thrust.

Last night, Tom, you drank wine with my wife.
You took my sons to see a movie
and then you went home alone. Alone.
You felt alone years ago, too,
proposed, indirectly, we share a bed.
I can't remember why
we didn't get around to it.

I had a visit tonight
and my family talked about you.
They brought you back to me with their stories.
Later, Maria and I sat under an oak tree

watching the kids play on the swings.
She told me how you have tried
to disappear in this unfriendly world.

The lovers are quiet now.
Their passions for the moment are sated;
they share the lingering warmth.
Soft laughter passes through the wall
like a nightbreeze.

If I could hold you maybe it would be easier.
But there are more than fences and guns now
to keep us apart.
All I can give you is this poem,
the body of poetry it belongs to
which is so much more than me.

The Question

Spring is in the forest.
Subtle shades of green, brown
and wildflower colours.
There are beginnings here, ends too.
It is a seasonal matter.
In this forest this spring
the oak on the clifftop groans
with the weight of change.
A rope burns into the bark,
the neck of the body it holds and
a beginning, or an end.

15

A CULHANE TRILOGY

The concluding entry on "Prisons" in the *Canadian Encyclopedia* reads:

> RELATIONSHIP TO COMMUNITY · Although generally isolated from the community, prisons depend on it for even a semblance of purpose and proper functioning. A network of interest groups with a variety of programs inside and outside the institutions has grown up around prisons, *e.g.* the John Howard Society and Elizabeth Fry Society, halfway houses, prison visitors and self-help groups. Citizens in general, however, tend to know little but seem to care less about what happens to people after they leave.

Claire Culhane is the most famous prison activist in Canada. Her indefatigable efforts on behalf of prisoners led to her being banned from prisons as a result of her involvement in the Citizens Advisory Committee during the hostage takings at the B.C. Pen in the 1970s. She has reminded the citizenry about who is in prison, what happens there and what happens to people afterwards. The following three excerpts trace Culhane's trials and tribulations as she fought for her right of entry into the prison system and argued eloquently and persistently for the accountability of that system to the citizenry. Claire Culhane died in Vancouver on April 28, 1996, after suffering a stroke. Tom Elton's tribute speech at her memorial service is a powerful testimony of Claire Culhane's legacy in the area of human rights.

The Grand Exit

Claire Culhane · 1979

It was now just five days since the last hostage went home. The Citizens' Committee had been monitoring, for twelve hours a day, various activities: to see that the Pen was returning to "normal"; to observe the movement of the 240 men from the destroyed East wing to the gym; to attend the Transfer Board sessions for removing eligible prisoners to other institutions; and to continue meeting with the Inmate Committee still lodged in the PTI area overlooking the gym.

At 8 A.M. my four-hour duty began. The Transfer Board was about to convene.

"Guess you're satisfied now you've given the inmates everything they asked for!" my escort jeered.

"Not exactly everything. But anyway, you have your two hostages safe and unharmed, haven't you?"

"We should've been allowed to do what we wanted to do in the first place," the guard persisted.

"And what was that?"

"Gas 'em!"

"And then what, after that?"

"There would've been no after that!"

It was still too early for the Board meeting. As my official ID-photo pass was not yet prepared, Jim Lazar (Living Unit Officer) took me to the gym area where I could talk with the I.C. I was still not allowed into the PTI area, so I had to talk with Gary Lake and others through the bars at the foot of the stairway. Six RCMP and Security guards were sitting at a table playing cards. No one bothered to search me, empty my purse, or use the metal detector.

Soon half a dozen prisoners had come to the gate to spell out their grievances. They needed garbage bags, toilet paper, clean laundry. A ton of putrid garbage at the exit gate had to removed. And then six or seven letters were handed to me for mailing to families to assure them everything was O.K.

> Ms. Culhane turned to six RCMP and a Pen security guard and asked what the procedure was about letters. No one seemed particularly interested and she got a shrug in reply... then asked the police and security "to please witness me accepting these letters and putting them in my outside pocket until I can drop them off at the V&C office."
>
> – *Vancouver Province,* Oct. 7, 1976

I didn't notice at the time that Lazar had quietly slipped away. Shortly, another guard came to take me back upstairs to the Transfer Board. There were many stories about the way prisoners were turned down without a chance to fully present and press their cases, so this was going to be interesting, to actually see for myself how the power play worked during direct confrontation between the Board and the prisoners.

It was not to happen.

Just as the first prisoner was called in, a guard suddenly asked me to follow him, this time to Security. We entered a waiting-room opposite the office of Mr. Ev Berkey (Acting Director of Security). He came in, accompanied by another officer apparently to witness Berkey asking me if I had any prisoners' letters on me. They were hanging out of my pocket, clearly visible. I handed them to him and started to explain the circumstances, but could get no further than the first few words.

> The prison controversy intensified Wednesday when Claire Culhane, a committee member, monitoring the clean-up at the B.C. Pen, was ordered to leave the prison for allegedly acting as carrier of inmates' letters. Prison officials confiscated a bunch of letters they said that they had seen being handed to Mrs. Culhane by some inmates.
>
> Jack Stewart (Information Officer) said letters handed in this manner are considered "contraband" and that ... Ev Berkey had ordered Ms. Culhane to leave the prison and told her not to come back.
>
> – *Vancouver Sun,* Oct. 7, 1976

My first reaction was just to sit down and refuse to move, confident that the accusation would be withdrawn if I had the opportunity to explain. However, there had been threats and innuendoes directed against the Citizens Committee in the past week; it was crucial that our group remain during this critical period, especially now that the Administration had sent the RCMP away. I realized they might use the letters to ban the entire Committee and thus weaken the prisoners' position.

I suffered the humiliation of allowing them to escort me out, but not until I made one more attempt to persuade Mr. Berkey to at least call Mary McGrath, who had similarly taken letters the day before. He side-stepped this, saying that he knew all about my "making posters for the prisoners," and that there were other "incidents" which he wouldn't specify.

The Administration was prepared to go to any length to maintain their control. An inquiring public was, and is, not wanted in the Pen, under any circumstances. If we couldn't be frightened away, we would be put out, one at a time if necessary, by fabrications such as these.

From *Still Barred From Prison*

Claire Culhane · 1985

My story began with my participation in the B.C. Penitentiary Citizens' Advisory Committee (CAC) during the 1976 hostage-taking, when it was learned that those in the Super Maximum area ("the Hole") were being hosed down and deprived of food, clothing and heat by the guards, who were venting their anger on the only accessible victims – the remainder of the prison was controlled by the Inmate Committee. It was incumbent upon the CAC to enforce the Letter of Understanding clause, namely, "to inform the public generally of conditions and issues arising within the institution." Not even after personally witnessing the wretched conditions could the Committee be persuaded to issue a press release. Following an unsubstantiated charge by the Administration that I had attempted to take prisoners' letters out, and the accompanying media furore, I was persuaded to resign from the CAC The alternative presented the possibility that the entire CAC might be asked to leave the prison at a time when its presence was crucial to the safety of the prisoners.

Two subsequent occupations of the Warden's offices to protest fresh violations of prisoners' rights resulted in convictions for criminal charges of illegal trespass of penitentiary land, and fines. My refusal to pay the fines resulted in their being written off. Shortly afterwards I was barred from further entry. Judicial measures to reinstate my visiting rights have yet to be tested in the Supreme Court of Canada. The ruling to bar me is enforced only in the Pacific Region (with a few exceptions). Even in the highest security levels, I am permitted to visit with prisoners everywhere else in Canada.

Far more ominous than members of the public being barred from entry into prisons is the pattern which emerges regarding the gradual but intimidating rendering of prisoners "incommunicado." The trend to curtail contacts leads to complete isolation during periods of crisis, including the denial of meetings with lawyers. It is in this context that citizens of Canada, analogous to other known repressive régimes, sometimes go "missing", particularly when prisoners are transferred before being able to notify their relatives. Security precludes answering distressed calls, and it is not until the transferred prisoners receive their personal effects (address book, stamps, stationery) that they can make the necessary contacts to advise where they have been moved.

The warning has been sounded consistently by every investigative body following various explosive situations that denial of legitimate contacts during such incidents can assume macabre dimensions.

From *No Longer Barred From Prison*

Claire Culhane · 1991

Not surprisingly, whenever anyone attempts to expose injustices in the prison system, the Administration's first step is to bar that person from visiting prisons. The following account of my success in recovering my visiting rights should prove instructive for any other friend or relative who may have been barred from visiting, without just cause.

Provincially

At the 1978 Proudfoot Royal Commission on Female Offenders at Oakalla, Judge Patricia Proudfoot was cautioned by myself that there really was no way she could protect witnesses – prisoners and guards alike – from reprisals against them on their return to Oakalla. When I concluded by saying that there could even be reprisals taken against myself for saying this, little did I realise what would happen so quickly. When I phoned Oakalla at lunch hour to confirm a pre-arranged visit with a prisoner, I was told that I was no longer permitted to visit or even telephone prisoners.

Not even a prompt call by Judge Proudfoot to the Administration and to the Regional Director succeeded in changing the Directive which barred me from visiting every B.C. provincial prison. No justification was required. My visiting privileges had been withdrawn on March 10, 1978, solely and allegedly "in the best interest of the Institution."

A word about the use of the term "privileges" as opposed to "rights" in relation to the status of prisoners and their visitors. In addition to the fact that not even courts of law can be depended upon to uphold clearly demonstrable and just demands by prisoners, such as the right to vote, the right to free (or otherwise) condoms, or the right to adequate medical attention, there is also a regulation whereby prisoners' visits shall be considered as a privilege, not a right, and may be suspended by action of the proper officials.

On May 19, 1987 I filed my petition under the Canadian Charter of Rights and Freedoms to have my visiting rights restored to prisons under the jurisdiction of the B.C. Correctional Service. Based on the Charter's recognition of the Rule of Law, the following sections were cited:

FUNDAMENTAL FREEDOMS

Section 2(b) "Freedom of Expression"

[Demand the right to express my concerns about the conditions in which the prisoners find themselves, without penalty of having my visiting rights withdrawn.]

Section 2(d) "Freedom of Association"

[Demand the right to associate with prisoners, which must include the right to visit them.]

LEGAL RIGHTS

Section 7 – "Everyone has the right to life, liberty and security of the person and the right not to be deprived thereof except in accordance with the principles of fundamental justice."

[Demand the right not to be deprived of my legal rights, based on Justice Lambert's judgement (B.C. Court of Appeal, 1980): ". . . the standards of fairness [as] requested by the Appellant [Culhane] are appropriate . . ."

EQUALITY OF RIGHTS

Section 15 – "Every individual is equal before and under the law and has the right to . . . equal benefit of the law without discrimination."

[Other groups and individuals who offer counselling and assistance are not excluded without cause. No information has ever been provided upon which this discriminatory action is based, which now prevents me from visiting prisoners in British Columbia. This restriction is not imposed on me, by any other Warden, anywhere else in Canada.]

A trial date was set for September 10, 1987.

The first response from the B.C. Corrections Commissioner was to permit me to visit all the Minimum security Camps in northern British Columbia, and if there was "no untoward incident" for the period of one year they might consider including Oakalla and the remaining Lower Mainland prisons.

However, I reminded the Commissioner that I was requesting that he immediately restore all my previous visiting privileges. Or, he could meet me in court.

The second response from the Commissioner, on September 1, nine days before the trail date, was an official confirmation that my visiting privileges were being restored. The trial was no longer necessary.

Federally

After having suddenly, within a one month period in 1980, been refused visiting rights by all eight Pacific Region prisons under the jurisdiction of the Correctional Services of Canada, for similar unspecified reasons and solely at the discretion of each Warden (two of whom opted to restore them following personal discussions), a Statement of Claim was filed against the remaining six on March 2, 1988 in the Federal Court of Canada Trial Division, once again declaring that this represented a denial of natural justice and a breach of duty to act fairly, contrary to the Charter of Rights.

A trial date was set for November 7, 1988 and once again visiting rights were restored just prior to that date, on the same basis as enjoyed elsewhere in Canada. I am permitted to visit as many prisoners in as many prisons as request my visit. [Although certain prisoners indicated their willingness to initiate their own legal action (to have access to their visitor), their offers were refused only because of my concern over possible reprisals against them.]

While I am aware of only one other person who is presently making use of the court procedures described above to restore her right to visit at a provincial prison from which she has been barred for no stated reason, I cannot let this moment pass without encouraging anyone who has been unjustly deprived of their visiting rights to also try to confront the authorities and have them restored.

Whenever they impede visiting, the Correctional Services must be held accountable for the undermining of family and personal relationships.

To the best of my knowledge (except for agencies such as the John Howard Society and the Elizabeth Fry Society), while other people are restricted to visiting one prisoner per institution and per region, I am the only private individual who is allowed to visit at every prison in this country. There should be others.

A Memorial to Claire

Tom Elton · 1996

Although the circumstances are saddening, having been given the opportunity to speak at Claire's memorial, I feel honoured – not because I've been chosen from what must've been a huge list of possibles, but because Claire so often spoke out on my behalf, and now I can give her some of that back by giving her my voice. So much can be said about Claire: her strength and self-dedication, her unalterable focus directed at the unjust and abusive, the fact she often fought harder for people than people fought for themselves. I'm sure everyone here has, in one way or another, experienced Claire's presence and strength of will in their lives. I'm also sure that (regardless of circumstance), that involvement proved beneficial.

Last week, some of Claire's friends gathered at Co-Op Radio to give tribute to a woman they knew and loved. That hour wasn't nearly enough! Today, we've four hours to tell our stories, share individual experiences so we all get to know the woman just a little better. And even these four hours will be too few; so much can be said about Claire.

Each of us has a particular Claire image, and though she hated being categorized or labelled – I've always had an image of Claire as *The Bringer of the Light* – I mean that in many different ways. The most effective way of bringing that image to you, I think, is by sharing some of my own, personal, Claire times. When I first met Claire I still had all my teeth, had never thought or worried about grey hair, and had never imagined my tattoos would one day sag. I was young, ignorant and a barbarian in every sense of the word: that was twenty years ago.

At that time I was on remand in Oakalla: a mutual friend asked her to visit and check on me. The fact the visit was conducted through "tapped" telephones with thick plexiglass sheets separating us was only part of the problem. That I could hardly string two consecutive thoughts together didn't help matters. And if that weren't enough to make our first meeting extremely difficult, my idea of being a conversationalist was limited to an occasional, monosyllabic grunt – it's a damn good thing Claire liked to talk.

Claire walked away from that visit knowing I was caught up in a complete and total sense of alienation. A week later she reappeared, bringing with her a woman I immediately fell in love with. The proverbial long days and nights were no longer an unending despair. Claire had brought me reason for emotional light and because of her it burned bright.

Claire's stories made me realize a world existed beyond my immediate experience, and that I knew little about that world. Listening to her made me painfully aware of *my* ignorance and *my* selfishness. Because of that it was easy for her to convince me I needed to go back to school – in itself that was a major accomplishment. Friends, before I was to begin, argued: "Why go to school? Don't do it, man." They warned: "They'll fuck up your head; you won't think the same; you'll quit hanging out with us." They were right, proving, I suppose, even barbarians have clairvoyant moments.

I went back to school, got my GED and then enrolled in the university program. Apart from the education and the wonderful people therein, I learned to think. And with thought came understanding: who I was, where I was and why I was there, and that if I thought my way through things – rather than simply reacting to them – I was as strong as (if not stronger than) the system confining me. Claire brought me the light of awareness.

Claire taught by example; lessons given were held in the classroom of the public eye. What made her specially effective was the fact she didn't care what others thought. She knew what was right and regardless of personal consequence, worked toward that. One of the lessons Claire taught me was about silence – just how dangerous a tool it is in the hands of the abuser. She encouraged me to write, goaded me to speak – showed me I had a voice and that people would listen.

In helping me develop a voice Claire gave me the means of self-protection, created an avenue through which I could help others; and gave me a weapon to battle things I believed unjust. It was then I came to recognize Claire's most powerful tool – her capability to *define* the system; she braced a faceless, nameless organism and gave it faces, names; she identified the separate components of the organism – individuals that can be held accountable for the things that go on – and made the struggle personal with / and to each one of them.

"It's important to know the people that run the prisons," Claire once told me. "It's them you'll have to deal with; people make the decisions, others carry out the actions. Make sure they know you, that you know them. Use your voice to get them to listen to their own inner voices. And always remember – never ever forget – it's the individual that can be held accountable, if not to the public then at least to themselves; make it personal!"

So much can be said about Claire, the least of which is that this world has become a better place because of her. Her absence now, in no way limits her presence – and though we will all miss her, we'll never lose her.

In closing, I'd like to tell you another little story, somewhat personal but relevant:

About a week and a half ago I was visiting my father, and told him that Claire had passed away and that I'd be going to some services.

"Will you be on the news?" he asked.

"Good possibility," I told him, "since I've been invited to speak."

He huffled, for a moment. "Well I'll just tell people that I don't know you, that you aren't my son."

I looked at him, somewhat shocked, somewhat angry, saw the twenty years of prison time I recently finished – all the times he wasn't there when I needed him, all the letters I never got. Then I realized that throughout those twenty years, no matter what the circumstances or where I was, Claire was there – filling that space of absence with visits and letters, with her Self. I think I can count myself very lucky; and I know I'm only one of so very many. And for that, and so much more, Claire, thank you.

16

DIRECT ACTION: THE SQUAMISH FIVE

In the summer and fall of 1982, a series of events occurred for which a group calling itself "Direct Action" subsequently claimed responsibility. These included the bombing of the Cheekye-Dunsmuir B.C. Hydro electric substation, the bombing of the Litton Industries plant in Toronto, and a number of arson attacks on outlets of the Red Hot Video pornographic video rental chain. In January of 1983, the RCMP announced that they had captured, on the Squamish Highway north of Vancouver, the "Direct Action cell" responsible for these actions. The police further indicated that this guerilla unit had planned a Brinks armoured car robbery, the sabotage of a Gulf Oil icebreaker, and an attack on the Canadian Air Force base at Cold Lake, Alberta. In 1984, after one and a half years of pre-trial imprisonment, the alleged members of "Direct Action" (the "Vancouver Five") were convicted of conspiracy to commit robbery; possession of explosives, unregistered weapons and stolen property; and the use of explosives. Ann Hansen received a life sentence, Brent Taylor twenty-two years, Julie Belmas twenty years, Gerry Hannah ten years, and Doug Stewart six years.

Interview with Gerry Hannah

John Abbott · 1984

Gerry Hannah was sent to Matsqui Federal Penitentiary in Abbotsford, British Columbia, where he was interviewed by John Abbott in the summer of 1984.

GH: I've always questioned authority, felt rebellious. I always questioned why others tell me what to do on a whim; that started at quite an early age. I could understand my mom telling me what to do, but . . . anyway I never really put my ideas into a sound political philosophy until I bumped into the anarchists in Vancouver, and then it clicked.

JA: It clicked when you went out and did something about it.

GH: Yeah, but it took me three years while I was doing my music, punk rock, before I got around to doing something about it. I never really intended to go underground, that was something that happened on short notice, like when the Litton bombing occurred and we found out that Julie's voice was on tape. Then it was a good time to disappear. Anyway, I guess it began for me after Julie and I moved to Jasper. We loved the Rockies and I wanted to work as a snow-cat operator. But it turned out that Jasper was the worst place to move to; it turned out that it was a completely sick little capitalistic commercial town. It really made me sick, dog-eat-dog. Things got worse and worse. I was driving truck, delivering at the cafeteria for the ski area. My boss was such a money-hungry slave driving jerk. His eyes just showed dollar signs. I'd thought that driving truck would be better than being a parking attendant, like sometimes it got down to 20 or 30 below. Driving, I thought, would be self-paced. But it turned out no way: there were no lunch breaks and whoever heard of coffee breaks? That and other things, frustrated me totally. We were trying to do it semi-straight, like everyone else, but we just couldn't. Not the way the rest of them up there make it, just hiking and such and not giving a fuck about anyone, just doing their own trip. I got fed up. . . .

I didn't really fit into society, I'd been a punk rock musician for three years. Never dreamed that I would be in this situation. And Carolin

Mines really upset me, the Coquahalla River Valley had been my boyhood tromping ground. I used to go up there and hike with my Dad. Now part of that watershed has been polluted with cyanide and whatever else the mine was dumping. Julie got a map of B.C. that showed environmentally endangered areas and there were projects and devastated areas all over B.C. I mean everywhere. And the Carolin Mine wasn't even included. It was big stuff like the Nechako Project and the Alice Arm mercury dumping into the sea where the local Indians get all their fish. They are turning B.C. into one giant industrial park. The whole place is going to look like New Jersey. The more I got exposed to this the madder I got. And I got exposed to hard core feminism when I met Julie.

JA: So meeting her was a real catalyst for change?

GH: Yeah. I quit the band after I met her. It was also the fact that I'm a woods person and punk is very urban. I had no time for the woods while I was in the band, on the road for three years. And Julie seemed the perfect mate, intelligent, politically aware, a feminist.

JA: And you didn't want to get in the rut of being established music.

GH: Yeah. I made a vow that I was to get out of the punk scene by the time I was twenty-six. The punk scene was against the old hacks, the dinosaurs of the music business, like Led Zepplin, Rod Stewart, The Dooby Brothers, who had become just other kinds of corporations, musical ones. Rock-and-Roll is supposed to be wild, alive and rebellious. Now the whole art of rock music is money. The recent bands even start out as old hacks, corporate groups like Boston and Aerosmith.

JA: Osterizer rock?

GH: Yeah. Music to them is just what formula will make it in the computer: should we mix some digital delay; some overdubbing; use a nice clean sound on the guitar; toss in some 50's, 60's or 70's riffs, let the computer decide what will be a hit. In 1977, when I started, punk was vehemently against the "boring old farts," the dinosaurs as we called them. I didn't want to be a thirty-year old player trying to hold onto my niche. That's why it is easier to let go. So I packed it in at the 1981 Anti-Canada Day Concert, my last concert, in Victoria, July 1st. A lot of things happened on Anti-Canada Day; the Subhumans started up then in 1978 and we ended it three years later. That was our day.

JA: And Julie got twenty years. Isn't that out of line with the six years that Doug got and your ten year sentence?

GH: That judge really nailed her. Doug and I didn't get hit with the Litton thing.

JA: I guess bombing the nuclear warhead guidance factory was hitting a little too close to home.

GH: The police reports were different on Julie and me, than on Brent, Ann and Doug. They don't think that we are that dedicated, but they feel that the others are very dedicated. Julie and I were planning on dropping the entire thing in a year. And anyway, the money was not just going to fund the guerilla work; Julie and I were going to use some of our shares to go live in the woods.

JA: Was the group a united organization, or what was its structure?

GH: It was a group dedicated to the philosophy of the urban guerilla. But it was an autonomous group. For example, the Cheekye-Dunsmuir bombing was done a month before I was involved. And at the time I didn't want to be involved in Litton, I was kind of swept away by it. That's not to say it wasn't OK. I agreed with the actions. It's just that I'm not suited for that kind of work. It is fine as part of the struggle but I should be into lower-key shit like raising people's consciousness; that's what I first started, what I really wanted to do in the first place. I wanted to do support work, maybe some low-level expropriation but not the high-level stuff. I didn't want to go underground.

JA: Would such reluctance explain why the group didn't carry out some of the more serious urban guerilla moves such as kidnap, assassination and fatal bombings like the Red Brigades, the Baader-Meinhof, or the IRA?

GH: Myself, I'm against terrorism. It's fucked up, even against the State, because they don't have any heart or soul and don't give a fuck about their own; there are always more cogs to fit into the machine, always more eager tools around. They just put on these shows of mourning for the public. No, I wasn't made for the urban guerilla lifestyle. It was a kind of relief to get arrested, like a huge weight was removed from my shoulders. Sorry to say it, but it's true; while it was happening I used to have nightmares, headaches, and get into all kinds of pointless arguments.

JA: What you have been saying here sounds somewhat like a book I read called *How It All Began,* by Bommi Baumann, the West German RAF member.

GH: Yes. That was the first book that Julie gave me. I'll have to read it again.

JA: So you would differentiate between the direct action of your urban guerilla and terrorism?

GH: Sure, we were careful not to kill anyone and we made it very clear that our actions were not of a terrorist nature. We wanted to educate, to show the people what could be done.

JA: You mentioned Berkman sometime back. Would you consider his attempted "attentat" or assassination against Frick as terrorism?

GH: Yeah, and it was political vengeance too. I mean I guess we could have ambushed Trudeau or something and a lot of people would have been secretly pleased, "ya, it's about time someone did something about that old fart," but there would have been a tremendous uproar against it publicly and that kind of action might have backfired. Now the Wimmen's Fire Brigade stuff wasn't terrorist action. It was an unexplored method in Canada of bringing attention to those questions. There was a consensus opinion not to be involved in assassinations. For lots of reasons, like none of us were too into doing it. It wasn't something which the public could relate to, and we already had little public support as it was. Anyway, until you remove the system there will always be someone else springing up, they're so brainwashed they think their sacrifice would mean something to corporate bosses. Things like the prosecutors and judges in Europe getting blown away by the Red Brigades I can sympathize with, but at best it is an act of revenge and, at worst, somewhat counter-productive. I can understand why, but personally I don't think that it is something that would be effective in Canada. In El Salvador, it's different. It is effective. If the Police Chief in the district is torturing and slaughtering the peasants and then someone assassinates him, well, there's a lot of popular support for that.

JA: Well, by the amount of time that the courts handed out to Ann, Julie and Brent, it looks like they viewed what did happen in the same light, pretty well as the same thing. I don't know if the judges draw those fine lines that you do between urban guerilla action and terrorism. Do you think that the courts have created martyrs with this sentencing, spreading the seed for future direct action?

GH: Yeah. Brent and Ann were blown out of the park, they're martyrs. The State described them as evil psychotics that led me astray. But you know there are a lot of women out there who didn't dig what happened to Ann. Somehow the people out there have to become aware that they are at war. That war was declared on the people with the creating of the State. Nuclear weapons, the destruction of the environment, the all-encompassing grab for profits and progress are just different fronts on which the war is being waged. That way we are all martyrs.

JA: From the sound of it, the women had a strong role to play, particularly Julie, for you.

GH: Yeah. I think the first time I saw her was at a benefit for "The Society of People Struggling to be Free." It was in support of Gary and Dino Butler. Our manager, a devout anarchist, got us involved. I started going to meetings of this Indian group. At the time Julie was another punk fan I saw at parties and demos but what caught my eye was that she showed up at the political meetings, like that one. Most punks just pay lip service to the political struggle side of it, just listen to the music but ignore the words; but here was a young woman right in the middle of things. I saw her again at the "U.S. Out of El Salvador" demo march; she was one of the organizers in the "El Salvador Support Committee." That impressed me a lot. I started talking to her at the march, ya me standing there like a big dumb punk while she was so busy, up to her armpits in work. That was the beginning of our relationship. When I went to her house, I immediately noticed the posters: most punk houses have a lot of punk posters on the walls and maybe a political one here and there, but she had more political posters, some really beautiful ones and just a few punk ones; ones about El Salvador, Survival Gatherings, European stuff and that environmental hazards spot poster of B.C. She is very intelligent and impressed the hell out of me.

JA: And the feminism?

GH: I went through some really drastic changes when I met Julie, about hard core feminism, she was very developed. She had spent a lot of time hanging out with female separatists...

JA: What does that mean?

GH: Well, the separatists have opted out of the whole male trip, they've said "Fuck It," men do nothing but mess up our lives so we're not going to have anything to do with them at all. Like they're serious about that too, for a while I was having doors slammed in my face, and found places where I wasn't welcome at all.

JA: Because you were a man?

GH: It was hard for me to understand too, but I can sympathize with it now because they have suffered pain I can't even realize. But it was hard for me. I can understand their trip: men do fuck over women, women are not subhumans, not fuck-bags good for nothing else. I've never been oppressed like women have been oppressed.

JA: Were you the big villain, anathema to the separatists, when you got together with Julie after her separatist experience?

GH: Well, we had lots of arguments, she was right 75% of the time: I was reacting with a lot of masculine attributes, using certain words, "chick" for example. These people insist that certain words are not to be used because of their connotations. It's not reverse prejudice. They have thought these things out and I respect it because it is important to them. Like, if someone kept calling me fuckwad and I asked them not to, well, if they respected me, they would respect my choice and not call me fuckwad. This stuff is based on reality and it comes from suffering so I had to change.

JA: So Julie helped politicize you, helped you develop in other directions?

GH: Yeah. I knew about the old-style anarchy while she knew a lot about modern guerilla warfare and feminist material. But I had the woods affinity. I'd been out there a good part of my life while she hadn't ever really been out there, so we complemented each other, it was a good mix.

JA: This picture is of Ann, isn't it? (Looking at the front page of the *Toronto Clarion*, 1984).

GH: Ann sure looks young in that picture, she must have been 26, or 27. She doesn't look the same at all now. The Red Hot Video bombing blew up in her face, she got horribly scorched. When I saw her the day after, I was sick. She was only standing a couple feet from the window when they funnelled the gas in: it blew back in her face.

JA: How about Doug? Did he start from the same punk rock direction?

GH: No, he never had anything to do with that. He was sort of a mystery man, a rabid environmentalist. He was part of the "Pacific Life Community," organizing against the Bangor, Washington, nuclear sub base. He did civil disobedience work, stuff with pamphlets. In some sense his feelings were stronger than mine about the environment, especially industrialism and its effects on animals. It deeply hurt him to hear of animals getting wiped out and the destruction of the natural world in B.C. He knew a lot about it too.

JA: The composition of the group is curious. Everyone came in from different directions.

GH: Yeah, but we shared a lot of things too. We were all anti-authoritarian people, anarchists. We believed in autonomous revolution; we shared that feeling too. We had a common concern about the environment. Brent was concerned more analytically about it, while Doug's was a more emotional concern. Brent was very well read: he knew all about the guerilla struggles in Third World countries. He was a political jack-of-all-trades, with his foot in every door. I specialized more in ecological concerns, though I wasn't involved in the Cheekye-Dunsmuir bombings. That was one of the things that attracted me to what was happening: someone was finally doing something. I didn't really have a chance to do anything in the group, I didn't do Litton because I chose not to and I was almost involved in the Red Hot Video arson, but by a stroke of fate I wasn't, even though I was convicted of attempting it. Most of the work I did was support, collecting things. The biggest collection of things was going to be the Brink's robbery, the bulk of my work was preparing for the robbery.

JA: Did you intend to take a direct part in the robbery?

GH: I fully intended to.

JA: So funding was a problem. Was it expensive going underground?

GH: Very expensive. We couldn't depend on working income. We weren't completely underground though. Doug was semi-underground; he still had someone outside the group who was regularly visiting him at his house. And Julie and I were still visiting my mother, we went there for Christmas, even had the dog along. It was only after a long time that I realized some of the intricate things that happened.

JA: Did you get a run-down of events when you joined up?

GH: No. I wasn't told a lot of things. We didn't tell each other stuff that we didn't need to know.

JA: Did the group just start with Ann and Brent?

GH: No. Doug was involved from the start. They had things going, but we didn't know what was happening. Julie and I were saying that we wanted to stop the corporations, hinder their Third World interventions. We talked about getting together and doing something about it, while they were sitting there having already done stuff.

JA: There must have been lots of glancing around.

GH: Plenty of giggling, but they kept a pretty cool secret, but then someone would show up with a piece, like a .45 or an M-IA and we would be totally surprised. "I didn't know you had that,", "Well, I do," period. It was a strange time. Julie and I didn't have many friends; we just couldn't relate to any of them. We were very cliquish, other people were intrusions into our world.

JA: Like aliens?

GH: Yeah. Very strange. And Doug is a very staunch feminist. He even, I think, found me a little repulsive, the macho overtones of punk clothes. I wore a lot of leather and I guess it seemed sexist to him. It was a joke to me because I was such a wimp, never fought anyone. So Doug was at first freaked out about that. You know, it was the whole commercial rock culture which drove me to the punk scene. The "Nifties" with their blow-dried feathered hair, nice cars and ski jackets, getting dressed up so that they could get laid. I started out with long hair, a beard, old cowboy boots and love beads, while my friends started wearing Adidas, they started following that mindless fad like sheep. Then when the punk look came along it seemed the perfect alternative. So we cut our hair: "long hair doesn't mean fuck all", punk had its shock value, saying to that scene "your trip is dead." I was very frustrated, always have been.

JA: What frustration? What would you like to do?

GH: I seem to fall into the same scenes that I hate. It is a constant struggle because I know what's wrong with it but slip into it anyway. And that's very frustrating, that's why I called myself Gerry Useless when I became a punk, to laugh at myself while having fun. To be rebellious and entertaining at the same time.

JA: Did Brent view the punk scene as a recruitment area?

GH: No. Nothing like that. He loves the fun and the wildness. Where the political thing is, he is. He likes that action. Brent really likes the punk scene. When we came back from Jasper, Julie was wondering what Brent was doing because she knew he wasn't a guy who would just sit on his ass. He said he wanted to do militant action and we got attracted to that. He could hardly say that he was already doing it. I had thought about being a hard-core revolutionary before, with the guns and all, even before I got politically developed. We talked about it a lot and gradually it became, over time, a more realistic possibility.

JA: How did you run into Brent?

GH: I knew Brent before. He was a local anarchist who put himself into the punk scene because it was by itself somewhat political. He felt it was good to see the young end of society involved in this, and Brent's been a person of action for a long time. We started seeing Brent a lot after we got back from Jasper, we shared many feelings about sexism, nuclear war, the environment. And there is this argument Brent and I get into: he says he became a guerilla because it was the next logical step to take after his activism, but he doesn't like it when I say I did it because I was frustrated. Brent says he was never frustrated by a lack of being able to get things together. I was looking for ways to deal dramatically with my frustration. As they say, punk rockers are just frustrated professional musicians.

JA: What does the term "underground" mean to you?

GH: It is a word that lumps all illegal fronts together: it describes the clandestine resistance groups either engaged in some kind of particular liberation struggle or militantly confronting the State on some issue.

JA: What are underground methods, for example?

GH: Well, stopping things through illegal means. One of them is direct action, direct confrontation with something, rather than taking the less direct routes such as sit-ins, die-ins, marches and demos, etc. Direct action is doing something yourself, instead of relying on someone or something else, like a political party, some group or some other structure that the State has sanctioned.

JA: So this is a personal decision?

GH: Yeah, but it is also a collective process, a smaller personal collective process.

JA: Do you have any ideas for other people interested in direct action?

GH: If there are any other underground groups in Western or Eastern Canada, the first consideration should be how far they want to go. This should be most carefully thought out. If they decide not to completely dedicate their lives to being an urban guerilla unit, their lifestyles should reflect that, keep their actions at a lower level than ours were. They should stay away from the sometimes cumbersome, sophisticated techniques that were used by "Direct Action."

JA: Well, describe some things that can be done on this lower level.

GH: This is an above-ground, transient level. For example, things like smashing windows in fur stores; this would be an action against the fur trade, spraying the furs with red paint. That's low level. Against B.C. Hydro or any other corporation that has equipment out doing damage to the environment, low-level groups could fuck with the equipment, slash the tires, put stuff in the gas. This is political vandalism: low-level direct action. On Grouse Mountain, citizens who didn't want the mountain logged hammered spikes into select trees so the lumber would be useless, it would destroy the expensive saws. Yeh, political vandalism.

JA: Isn't this kind of thing easily curbed by the corporations, more wire, dogs and security guards, etc.?

GH: No. If enough people do it, if they have a strong support group, if they keep it up, well the project becomes too expensive. Since that's the whole point of the corporations, profit, they will stop. It has worked. One of the advantages to this type of action is that it is easier to attract people to do it. The community is less apt to misinterpret the motives of those involved and it involves less risk and less consequences if one gets caught. Whereas when people decide to go high-level they should go completely underground from the start. Totally. That is the first ground rule. There can be no compromise on that.

JA: Do you feel there is a role for high level guerilla activity in B.C.?

GH: There is a role for it anywhere in the world. If the goal is revolution, a much misinterpreted word, a complete change in society, away from the exploitation/domination to a collective sharing, there is no way to avoid what some would call violent acts. There have to be a lot of people involved and there has to be a lot of support. Some might say that there isn't that support in B.C., but the groundwork has to be laid now for the armed resistance which has to come.

JA: What kind of groundwork?

GH: The idea that guerilla activity is a useful tool in raising political consciousness, in resisting the State, has to be put on the table for discussion now. That's what we did. The examples have to be looked at now because we don't have time, the world may be destroyed tomorrow by global nuclear war and total environmental collapse. If we don't take care of the planet we won't be around to liberate anyone: women, oppressed minorities, anyone. That's why the environment has to be dealt with now. We're are losing the life of the world, its oxygen generating forests, huge areas every day. That's why the environment is my top priority.

JA: Do you believe other people in B.C. should take up high-level guerilla activity?

GH: Yes. If they feel they could be doing it. I don't feel right in recommending it to others while I have given up on that level of struggle myself. For some people it is a good idea if they are that type of person. We're never going to change things enough without forcibly removing certain elements in our society who have the power. They have everything and they'll never just give it away. They also, unfortunately, have the means to brainwash the public to believe they're helping them when they're actually robbing them. It is going to be very difficult but it has to happen. I still support revolution totally although I am a retired guerilla now.

17

CONVOCATIONS

In 1972 university programs were introduced into the B.C. Penitentiary and were highly successful. The Valedictorian addresses of Frank Guiney and David Turner testify to fundamental changes brought about by the educational process. The changes are at once highly personal and a part of a larger collective achievement as the student body defined itself in ways very different than those imposed by the prison structure. Frank Guiney's "Humanities at Main and Hastings" talks about the "social prisons" with their "invisible walls" which enclose so many in the East-side of Vancouver. Guiney, the ex-prisoner, taught SFU sponsored courses at the Carnegie Centre and discusses the impacts of these offerings on the students. As Malcolm Lowry stated in his poem on Hastings Street, "Christ Walks in this Infernal District Too":

> And on this scene from all excuse exempt
> The mountains gaze in absolute contempt,
> Yet this is also Canada, my friend,
> Yours to absolve of ruin or make an end.

Valedictorian Address: B.C. Pen, 1976

Frank Guiney · 1976

Ladies and Gentlemen; Honoured Guests; Faculty Members; and My Fellow ...what? How should I address my fellows? Should I say, Fellow Students? Or should I say Fellow Prisoners? I suppose this matter of self-identification reflects one of the difficulties I encounter in considering what to say to you today. Because, after all, we are prisoners. Yet, it cannot be denied that we are university students. As of today, we have the papers to prove it.

So do I talk to you today, on behalf of my fellows, as a student...or as a prisoner? Perhaps it is trite to say that people tend to live up to their labels ...but nevertheless there is much truth in the statement. The observation is rather important, at least to me, because outside this room...out there ...all around us...is functioning a sick monstrosity... a prison...where society tries to hide all its problems and mistakes; the complete abnormality in which we live ... except for a few hours out of the day, thank God, when we can leave it and come here. At least that's how I feel.

It is difficult for me, and I think, for my...fellows...to forget that. So it is a temptation to speak to you today as a prisoner, to identify with that label.

Then too, we who are enrolled in the university are only some thirty people...which means there are some four hundred other...labels out there. And I cannot speak to you without, in some way, speaking for them also. What I say here cannot help but concern them.

I do not intend to hold any briefs here today. I have no interest in bitching and grousing or twisting the lion's tail . . . I simply wish to point out to you that I have much difficulty at this moment separating my two identities.

If I talk to you as a prisoner, I'm sure I would be inclined to emphasize the negative aspects of our existence. I have nothing, repeat nothing, good to say about prisons. They are sick; they are useless; and they are destructive.Not even with the very real sense of gratitude I feel for the presence of this university program can I find it in my heart to say anything good about prisons.

In these rooms, you see, for a few hours a day, five days a week, is contained one of the few breaths of fresh air available to us. These rooms, to us, are somehow . . . not really part of the prison.

Oh, we don't forget that we are locked in here securely every day, and God knows we encounter plenty of frustrations on the other side of that barrier, just getting here, and staying here, the prison routine does not bend much to suit the university purpose. But in these rooms we have an opportunity to talk differently . . . to think differently . . . maybe we even act differently.

In the university area it's a different ball game. Almost like taking on a different identity every day. I think, too, from what I see here from day to day, and from month to month, that people who come into this program very often surprise themselves, in that they discover they are capable of much more than they had imagined; that their thinking and their attitude toward many things in the world, including themselves, can broaden and change enormously.

Oh, I'm not going to lay any nonsense on you about people suddenly "turning over a new leaf." I personally think it is naive and unrealistic to speak of any adult human being turning over a new leaf. I believe people have life-styles; and those life-styles are formed early and remain pretty consistent. At the same time, I think that an individual's functioning, within that life-style, can be very much affected by inner growth, and I think that inner growth is inevitable as a side-effect of university education.

And I don't think that a particular life-style, whatever it is, need bring anyone back to jail. Human beings are flexible and resilient . . . especially the young . . . and given that awareness and inner growth I speak of, they can develop ways and means of meeting the social complexity, regardless of life-style.

My lawyer, who is also a friend, is here today. I suppose my presence here may not appear as the best advertisement for his legal expertise, and I hope he is not embarrassed by it . . . I assure you, the score, in this case, is no indication of the play . . . In any event, some fourteen months ago, when we were waiting for the jury to decide where I would be taking my room and board for a while, he asked me how I felt about things. I told him then that I felt like Canada's oldest living Juvenile Delinquent.

Today I have this certificate . . . which I should have obtained when I was nineteen or twenty. That's progress. Now I am forty-three, going on twenty. Do you know where I was when I was nineteen? Right down the hall, serving my first sentence here. There wasn't any university program in those days.

So you see, my feelings about all this are kind of ambivalent. As a prisoner, I loathe this prison, and all the prisons it represents. Prisons produce little else, in my opinion, than prisoners. The prison experience trains people to think like prisoners, to act like prisoners, and to react like prisoners. That is the deadly paradox that society has set for itself. Society lays an impossible task on prison administrators, expecting than to produce normal people while forcing them to conform for long periods of time to an abnormal environment. It can't work. It is an exercise in futility.

At the same time, I would be less than honest if I said I was not grateful for this university program . . . consciously, personally thankful that it is here. I just want to make it abundantly clear that I think the university program survives in spite of, not because of, the prison.

As a prisoner, I am sure no one expects me to extoll the virtues of those who are charged with keeping me here. As a student, I must thank the people who work to keep the university program here; to keep this little island of non-prison life open to us; and hopefully to expand it.

Valedictorian Address: Mountain Institution, 1985

David Turner · 1985

We speak from experience when we say attaining graduation was a series of small steps, years, semesters, days and, sometimes, even hours. Each was attained in its own way, each in its own time.

To know exactly how we feel here today, you would have had to experience the frustrations, the failures, the desire to quit and walk away.

There were many times when the stronger of us would help the weaker, only to have the roles reversed weeks later. We know we gained our degrees through hard work, but more importantly, we learned to give and take of ourselves in the process.

This truth is brought home if we stop and ask, Would I be what I am today if there wasn't someone there when I needed them to talk me out of quitting, someone there when the pressure got too much, someone telling me to dig deeper within myself for the strength I never knew I had?

The last point I wish to make is, without a doubt, the most important. This program exists, survives, on the premise that it brings change to the individuals who participate within it. If this were not true I sincerely doubt we would be here today.

I have read the literature on this program and I can tell you with all sincerity that it delivers what it promises.

Those of you who know me from before will recognize that my changes speak for themselves. The more difficult task is to illustrate how I became who I am.

To do this I must borrow from the writings of John Donne. Three hundred and fifty years ago Donne wrote that: "Any man's death diminishes me."

Four years ago this statement would not have elicited further thought. Not only would I have failed to understand what was being said, I would not have cared. Today I understand. Today I have learned that any man's death makes me smaller, less than I was before. I now know this because I now know that the world is an infinite map of interconnections.

Today, I have come to understand that everyone represents a world within themselves, a world full of wonder, excitement and surprises. We are all souls full of mystery and love. Whenever anyone dies, a planet is destroyed. Messages of condolence should be flashed across the galaxy.

Regretfully, in my studies of humanity I have also found reason for sadness and it speaks highly of the program that I would even notice. This becomes apparent whenever suffering or tragedy surfaces.

I used to think that feelings of human sympathy were something I dusted off whenever tragedy was brought to my attention on the six o'clock news. Today I know that it is something I am blessed with all the time.

I can no longer feel only for deaths of significance, but also now for the sufferers who are closer at hand, for the family down the street whose plight goes unnoticed and untelevised, for all those whom I might actually help.

My education was expensive and now I have an obligation to help where I can.

The fact that we are educated within a prison, separated from the community by time and space, has served to enhance our concept of humanity elsewhere and yet always in relation to ourselves.

In his book *Language and Silence*, George Steiner notes that he was perplexed to consider how the torture and murders committed at Treblinka could be occurring at precisely the same time that people in New York were making love or going to the theatre.

Were there two kinds of time in the world, Steiner wondered. Good times and inhuman times?

It is a question such as this which lends itself to the lessons found in our study of the humanities. To become more humane is to discover the relations between inside and outside, between those dying and those alive when death occurs and the relation of all three to ourselves.

There may not be two kinds of time in the world, but there does seem to be two kinds of sympathy: one that weeps and disappears and one that never leaves the watch.

I know now that sympathy, unlike pity, must have some application to the future. Humanities has taught me that if I do not feel deeply the suffering I am powerless to prevent, how would I be alert to the suffering I might put an end to?

A very dear friend gave to me a remarkable definition of nobility. It holds special significance for those new students who are seeking a better understanding of what to expect from this program.

Mr. Douglas Haines once told me that "True nobility is never found in being superior to someone else, but rather, it is found in being superior to one's former self." In this regard we three graduates can now claim nobility, true nobility.

In closing, I would like to share a short, but meaningful, prayer. These words were first spoken by a newly emancipated slave, over 120 years ago, but the spirit is especially appropriate today. It is not a prayer for a bowed head, but rather for a raised head. It goes:

Dear Lord, I ain't what I should be,
And I ain't what I'm going to be,
But thank you Lord, I ain't what I used to be.

Humanities at Main and Hastings

Frank Guiney · 1984

To paraphrase and possibly to twist a well-worn cliché: our society does not require stone, concrete, barbed wire, steel, and gun towers to manufacture its prisons. As any student of social anthropology or urban geography knows, there are number of barriers, social, economic, ethnic, and educational, to name a few, which can imprison people as effectively as the more visible variety of walls and wire mesh.

The Downtown Eastside Core of Vancouver may be seen as a prime example of a "social prison" created by invisible barriers. Enclosed within an area most often referred to as Vancouver's "Skid Road", implying, of course, that those who live there are all bums, drunks, drug addicts, and prostitutes, are thousand of ordinary people locked into their immediate environment with little means to attempt escape.

Certainly, the Eastside Core contains significant numbers of alcoholics, drug users, hustlers, and others who occupy ostensibly self-imposed positions on the bottom rung of the social ladder. But, aside from the fact that many of these social pariahs are actually products, self-fulfilling prophecies produced by the social prison itself (and any long-term prisoner behind visible walls can testify to the debilitating effect that prolonged imprisonment can wreak on an otherwise healthy psyche), aside from that consideration, the fact is that the majority of residents in the Downtown Eastside are not drunkards and addicts and prostitutes.

The greater percentage of its population consists of old age pensioners, handicapped people, unemployed workers subsisting on U.I.C. and Welfare, many with a stunned look in their eyes. They wonder how the years of their working lives, producing, paying taxes and union dues, raising families and contributing their sweat and expertise to their society, have brought them to this: standing in a food line three blocks long to get a sandwich, staring down at the sidewalk, hiding their faces from the TV cameras seeking out the sensational stories about the "Skid Road." They don't look too much different than the lines of convicts at "feeding time" in the old penitentiaries.

Another segment of the population is just plain down-and-outers who, for one reason and another, never did get a crack at the upward mobility that could get them over the invisible walls of the Downtown Eastside perimeter . . . legally.

A few people stay in the area by choice, most by necessity. Where else to live for a young unemployed high school drop-out collecting $325 to $375 maximum largesse from the welfare coffers? A 12 × 12 room for $200 a month in any other area of Vancouver would be a lucky find, indeed.

Obviously, not everyone in similar straits gravitates to the Eastside Core. Many people pool their resources and share accommodation in more attractive surroundings. But some people, again, for various reasons, cannot or prefer not to resort to such arrangements and simply survive as best they can, as any prisoner does, within the invisible walls, striving to retain their identity.

Another similarity to prison life is the cell-like atmosphere of many of the tiny Eastside hotel rooms which lack access to any nearby recreational facilities. Once the balance of the welfare money is gone after the rent is paid, which is usually early in the month at today's food prices, even the relaxation of nursing a couple of draft in one of the hotel bars is a financial impossiblity. Apart from walking the street or sitting at a bus stop bench, the bars constitute, of course, the main source of a "place to go" to escape the 12 × 12 room.

Originally a library, then a museum, Carnegie was saved from the developers and the wrecking ball some 4 1/2 years ago by the Downtown Eastside Residents Association (DERA). Many programs, facilities, and services have since been initiated at Carnegie for Eastside residents, mostly through the involvement of volunteer workers.

Recently Carnegie Centre introduced something new to its list of programs: educational opportunities for poor people. To explain the far reaching implications of this innovation, I must return briefly to the comparison between invisible social prisons and the more visible walled-in variety . . . both of which our society would prefer to hide away and ignore.

Two points seem salient here. The first is that one of the destructive influences of living in a social prison is analogous to that experienced by many long-term penitentiary inmates. In the beginning, a prisoner "makes the best of it", which of course leads to "getting used to it." One starts thinking of oneself as a prisoner, lives up to the label of prisoner, maintains the mind-set of a prisoner, accepts the limitations and boundaries that go with being a prisoner. Human beings tend to live up (or down) to the labels imposed upon them.

I have talked to many people who live in the Carnegie area (I prefer the term to "Skid Road") who say quite candidly that they have reached the point where they are not interested in "breaking out." They don't care to attempt escape. They are content to stay in the Carnegie area. A number of these people have simply given up. The rut has become familiar, relatively "comfortable." Finding and fighting for the means of escape, the tools to carve out a way to equality and social justice, have become exercises in futility. They will settle for what they've got, and make the best of it.

Other, long-time residents, simply prefer living in the area. They like the atmosphere. All their friends are in the Downtown Eastside Core. Socializing or living beyond the perimeters would be a discomfort; they would feel out of place; "out there" people live differently, have different interests, even talk a different language, as it were.

Still others talk about wanting a job and the chance to move out, but in these days of depression-figure unemployment, few jobs are available, and an objective observer frequently gains the impression that few people, even highly skilled tradesmen in the social prison, actively look for work. Initiative has become limited; ambition has dissipated. Many seem to have crossed the line between "making the best of it" and "getting used to it." The expressed desire to "get to work, get off welfare, get a better place to live, if only I could find a job," often sounds like the rationale that goes with seeing yourself as a hopeless case.

I can offer little hard evidence, but I believe that the debilitating experience of downward mobility from productive working person to UIC recipient, to Welfare case, to entry into the population of the social prison, engenders the loss of dignity which produces the loss of self-esteem and then the stunned expression and the look of resignation I see in people's eyes. If you are told you are a hopeless case often enough, you will begin to believe and act like a hopeless case.

My second point is that the Carnegie area is composed of many people, young and old, who dropped out of the elementary or high school systems before they fulfilled their real potential. Perhaps they dropped out for economic reasons, perhaps because they were "turned off" by the system . . . any number of reasons. (One Native Indian man told me that his missionary school teachers advised him he would be "unwise" to go beyond Grade 9. He later went on to Grade 12, in spite of the advice and became a journeyman electrician).

Many of the people in the social prison in the Carnegie areas have completed Grade 12 in regular high school: many have upgraded their education to Grade 10 or 12 in "equivalency" courses, in hopes of enhancing their employment opportunities (or, in some cases, to get a few extra dollars a month from welfare).

But a significant proportion of the Downtown Eastside population are people who are "long on life experience and short on formal education."

In any event, for all these people, the notion of ever doing university-level work was, until a few months ago, a far-fetched notion indeed.

Even for people outside the walls of the social prison I have attempted to describe, recent government cut-backs in education at all levels, and the government attitude toward education, especially education for poor people, have begun to turn the universities in British Columbia into institutions for the elite, the upper classes who can afford it. Certainly, there is little hope for higher education for residents in the social prison.

But a breach has been made in the invisible walls.

Simon Fraser University's Institute for the Humanities, through Dr. Stephen Duguid, recently came up with an innovative idea to bring university-level education to the Eastside community.

Duguid had designed and written a special curriculum for use in university programs in Federal Penitentiaries. The curriculum, a Humanities Core Curriculum (HCC), is entitled "Human Nature and the Human Condition" and is meant to fulfill a variety of purposes, one of which is to serve as a preparation course or "gap filler" to acquaint students with university work. Discussion based, the course has as one of its attributes the fact that it is accessible to people who may be short on formal education but who, along with life experience, have the ability to read, analyse issues in condensed excerpts from famous scholars, philosophers, and writers, and then formulate and express their views and opinions orally (and, if capable, in writing).

Duguid proposed this idea to Carnegie's Director, Nancy Jennings. Jennings had been one of the advocates and originators of an educational program in the Community Centre and had persuaded Vancouver Community College's (King Edward Campus) Department of Continuing Education to provide part-time funding for a Learning Centre Coordinator to work with volunteer tutors who would bring free educational assistance to people in the Carnegie area. The facility offered tutoring at almost all levels, general help, advice, referrals, courses in English as a Second Language and Conversational French, and upgrading encouragement among its variety of programs.

The Carnegie Learning Centre became a reality in November, 1983. Duguid found out about it in March, 1984.

Long a believer that university education should be made more accessible to people in the community and with Simon Fraser already establishing downtown university facilities in Vancouver, he discussed with this writer the viability of bringing university level studies to Community Centres. We both see similarities in the problems confronting residents in the "social prison" and those which many penitentiary prisoners describe as factors which brought them to jail. We decided to take a chance and offer the Humanities course at Carnegie as a pilot project.

Would there be a significant response from the Carnegie community and fringe area? Would local residents demonstrate the wherewithal and determination to stick with a non-credit university course with no tangible reward, just the accomplishment itself and a certificate of completion? Would people, many of whom lived through the many days wondering where their next hot meal would be found, see the value in foregoing the peace, diversion, and recreation offered in other programs, to study the readings and spend three hours in class discussion? Would only a handful of people sign up initially, and only one or two finish?

Oddly enough, many of the pessimistic questions asked were almost identical to ones that were asked when the first university courses were brought to B.C. Penitentiary some 12 or 13 years ago. Could we make it succeed at Carnegie?

Duguid would supply the course from his Humanities Core Curriculum. Carnegie would supply the space. I would supply my services as instructor. The course would be offered free.

The course was advertised by poster in three locations for five days: The Carnegie Centre, a local Welfare office, and the Vancouver Indian Centre. An "Information Session" was held on March 24. Twenty-six people attended. Twenty-five enrolled in the first section of the curriculum, title "The Individual and Society." By the time the first class was held a week later (March 21) another five people had signed up. The response had far exceeded our most optimistic estimates. We had to split the class in two.

Over the next 12 weeks we had a 43 per cent drop out rate, most of them in the first 2 to 3 weeks. On June 30, 17 people finished the course. On July 15, a "ceremony" was held, and the Director of the SFU Institute for the Humanities presented 11 people with certificates. The other six received letters of congratulation for their efforts.

Since then, two "graduates" have enrolled in College courses. Another was accepted as a mature student at UBC. Refusal for a student loan, however, stymied his efforts, but he still intends to get to university somehow. Another certificate recipient is writing a play. One has started a book. Eight people from the pilot project have continued into the next section of the curriculum, and 14 are working in the introductory section used in the pilot project.

At this writing, we are completing the two Carnegie courses and another pilot project at Westgate in the Lower Mainland Regional Correctional Centre (Oakalla). From the class of 16 university students at Westgate, one prisoner was recently paroled. He attended the university class at Carnegie the next day so he might finish the course which, fortunately, has been running at the same pace as the Westgate project. The parolee intends to attend the next semester at Simon Fraser. Another prisoner at Westgate is due to be released in a few days and will complete the course at Carnegie, also. His intention is to apply for admission to Pacific Vocational Institute.

I am no "-ologist" of any kind, but for me one of the most interesting experiences has been in presenting these pilot projects, one "outside" and one "inside", and noting little difference between the Westgate prisoners' performance and some subtle changes in attitude and demeanor, and those of the people I envisage as living within the invisible walls of the Carnegie area.

My mandate has not been to rehabilitate, only to instruct, but I truly believe that I have seen the university experience contribute something to an awakening search for freedom in both restricted environments in some people. Again, I have no hard evidence, other than the people who have gone on to continue higher education efforts (which admittedly, they may have done anyway), but I have detected a different look in some people's eyes and I have noted changes in their topics of conversation, which to me looks like a gain in self-esteem.

At the risk of being labelled too much the optimist, I entertain the hope that some of these people have found in themselves at least the potential for a means of escape, from behind the invisible walls of the social prison, as well as the walls we can see.

18

POSTSCRIPTS

In the cover letter for his Foreword, Robert Kroetsch wrote: "And what a loss – that educational program." Instead of future "convocations", callings together, there would now be a silencing of voices in terms of the demise of university programs in Canada's prisons. No longer would a humanities-based curriculum test and confront the very ethos of the prison, thereby assisting in the raising of questions of concern to all of us about the very nature and function of prisons, a dialogue conspicuous only by its absence in this country. Ironically enough, at the very time that the CSC was beginning to cancel post-secondary programs in 1991, it was still circulating a pamphlet extolling the virtues of such programming: "The provision of such post-secondary educational opportunities recognizes that inmates must become as complete human beings as they can. They must have an increased understanding of themselves, of their fellow citizens and of the world in which they will eventually live and work." In the termination letter sent to Dr. Evan Alderson, the Dean of Arts at Simon Fraser University, March 24, 1993, M.J. Duggan, Deputy Commissioner, Pacific, stated: "As we identify and priorize the needs of our offender population, we conclude that we must reallocate our scarce resources to priority needs such as programming for violent offenders and substance abusers which more directly target the criminogenic factors facing offenders." Here in Duggan's "postscript" is laid out the corpse of university programming in Canadian prisons, awaiting an autopsy or critical dissection. The always handy excuse of budget shortfalls hardly bears scrutiny since the monies allocated for university programming were minuscule to say the least in terms of the CSC bottom line. In the Spring of 1998, the CSC announced it was hiring over one thousand new correctional officers; not one new hiring was made for either educators or social workers. No, what is really central here is the underlying assumption that university programming is not "core" to the CSC mandate, that it is only a frill that can be dispensed with. But the inescapable and fundamental point is that there was no reason why university programming could not have co-existed with the CSC's new programming initiatives. Wayne Knights' post-mortem reflections on the cancellation of the Program at William Head Institution and his letter to the editor and that of a student in the Program, Bob MacDonald, raise these and a number of other related issues. Perhaps their comments as well as my concluding remarks on a visit to the old B.C. Penitentiary site will contribute to further discussion of the role university programming played in Canada and the benefits it so obviously offered to prisoners. The quixotic tilting at prisons has to go on.

Death on the Installment Plan

Wayne Knights · 1993

The news of the cancellation of the university program was in the prisons before any official announcement was made. A team of auditors arrived at William Head Institution and casually mentioned it to a group of managers.

The supervisors in charge of programs were so upset they informed me unofficially, asking only that I not tell the students. I pointed out that it was just a matter of time before they knew once staff were told. They agreed. I phoned my counterparts at Simon Fraser and the other prisons, met with the students, and we began to plot our Waterloo.

We had a model to draw on. In 1983, when the program was cancelled, we had successfully reversed the decision. The strategy was simple: flood the Solicitor-General's office with letters of support and petitions, seek publicity for our case and editorial support from newspapers, and rally support from adult educators, criminologists and members of the criminal justice system nationally and internationally. It took a year, but we were victorious. We did all the above. However, well before March 1993 two of our campuses had already been closed down, and we had failed to defend them – partly because they were largely comprised of sex offenders. By allowing corrections to split General Population and Protective Custody inmates from each other and their common interest we were already at a disadvantage.

Other things had changed too. In 1983, we had the covert support of corrections managers at the institutional and regional levels and we had a recently completed study to buttress our case in the media. Although we had developed a significant international network of support in the world of correctional education, we lacked local influence. And finally, we were up against a Conservative government during its last hurrah, cutting and slashing, desperately trying to win electoral support from a disaffected public. Playing the crime card, with its appeal to law and order, punishment and discipline, was as inevitable as their own demise.

More insidiously, government had modelled itself on business management. Armed with a "mission statement" and a programming ideology to support it, it was time to be efficient, targetting individual clients to meet specific needs. The vision of the prisoner as both a consumer and a commodity is representative of the ideal core of historical experience, if opinion-makers are to have their way. Lately, they have.

According to a staff member in the Solicitor-General's Office, we drove them nuts. But we failed (Waterloo redux). When the university program finally shut down, the prison, having rejected the virus of independence and creativity it tried to embody, was left to pursue its dream of a rationalized, dessicated and orderly program of experience for clients.

Valuable Program Cut

Wayne Knights · 1993

Published as a letter to the editor, the Toronto Globe and Mail, *April 30, 1993*

How ironic that while the federal government considers adopting a "Federal Learning Strategy," it chooses to discontinue the highly successful university program administered by Simon Fraser University in federal prisons ("For a Federal Role in Education", editorial, April 14). For 20 years this program has offered post-secondary adult education to inmates in B.C. It has retained the popular support of inmates, proved cost-effective, and it has gained international recognition. In addition, a correctional service pamphlet on post-secondary education cites research indicating that it also meets the Service's rehabilitative mission.

Not surprisingly, inmates typically have dropped out of school, and thus possess high illiteracy rates and all the other characteristics that so concern top-level strategists. Indeed, one correctional official has called the prison "a cognitive slum." Efforts have been made to address educational needs to the Grade 10 level, but to leave inmates to the vagaries of the job market with that qualification tucked in their back pocket would seem to be irresponsible from the "crime fighting" point of view.

The Simon Fraser University program has been an innovator in this field for two decades, primarily by addressing prisoner education through carefully thought-out programming. Thus it has developed peer tutoring and upgrading programs to the university level, integrated correspondence courses and on-site learning, provided counselling and transitional services to post-secondary institutions of all types, as well as offering university-level courses in the humanities and social sciences. A few students even managed to complete their BA degrees while incarcerated, but this is not the primary goal of the program.

To quote the federal strategy paper, building a "grassroots learning culture" in the prison is a good description of the real goal. So why pursue a national strategy if local initiatives are going to be eliminated? The provinces should be concerned.

Killing prison's SFU program a giant leap backwards

Bob MacDonald · 1993

Published in the Victoria Times-Colonist, *May 12, 1993*

Beginning July 1, 1993, post-secondary education will end at William Head Institution. The decision to cut the Simon Fraser University Prison Education Program has apparently been made in response to budget restrictions. One wonders, however, whether a program with a 21-year record of success is a reasonable and judicious cut. Could budget reductions have come from another area? Will the elimination of higher education mean reduced spending?

The Pacific Region Co-ordinator of Inmate Programming says post-secondary education is the obvious area to cut since it will have the least negative effect on the Correctional Service of Canada mandate. Harold Golden also says the public disagrees with the prisoners receiving university education. He expresses the hope, somewhat sarcastically, that inmate students would use their newly learned critical thinking skill to understand the cuts.

The implication that prisoners receive a "university education" is somewhat misleading. It is true that some have earned degrees, but the majority receive first- and second-year instruction in humanities and liberal arts. Others complete degree programs after release, at their own expense. The awarding of degrees is not and has never been the focus of the program.

Golden may find the public not as disagreeable as he might hope. He may recall that the Liberal government cancelled the program in 1983 only to reverse the decision under the weight of public protest. There are also serious doubts as to whether its elimination will mean reduced spending.

When Deputy Warden Dan Dennis announced the end of post-secondary education, he hinted that Corcan Industries would be established at William Head, adding wistfully that prisoners would "build things." If true, any talk of budget cuts is fraudulent. The so-called reduction is a shift away from education to industries where prisoners are trained to perform jobs that do not exist outside the prison. Corcan would employ about half the number of prisoners currently enrolled in university courses and cost more to operate.

Corrections officials will say that Corcan is a special operating agency with its own budget and that the cost of the university program comes from yet another budget. All the budgets, however, come from the same pocket. Any accountant using these bookkeeping methods might find himself "building things" at William Head.

The most ludicrous part of Harold Golden's statement is that cutting the SFU program will have the least negative effect on the CSC mandate, part of which is to prevent recidivism. A major study of the Prison Education Program indicates a recidivism rate of only 16 per cent. The rate from all other programming, including industries, literacy and mandatory treatment programs, is four times as high. Since a program with an 84 per cent success rate is being discontinued, we might logically conclude that CSC's mandate is to increase recidivism.

Many people have tried to squeeze theories out of the success of the university program. Some say it reduces cognitive and moral deficits, others say it opens the mind and broadens the horizons. No doubt there is a degree of truth in all of these proposed theories.

We must not, however, think of "prison education" as though it were a corrective thing designed to fix broken people. We should instead think of "education in prison" and accept the fact that a liberal arts education has an intrinsic value of its own and just happens to have a rehabilitative aspect. Let us stand on the record of success.

Canadian taxpayers recently spent $8.2 million for new living units at William Head. The design emphasized integrated living, where prisoners do for themselves rather than have things done for them. With this concept Canada leads the world in penology. Time alone will gauge its success. The CSC has now decided to cancel the international model for prison education, at the same time it is retaining and increasing funding for programs that are demonstrated failures. Sadly, on July 1, this forward-looking institution will take a giant leap ahead into the past.

Coffee at 'The Pen'

P.J. Murphy · 1994

To be visiting the B.C. Penitentiary site for the first time some fourteen years after its official closure did seem strange, a kind of post-mortem that revived a host of memories since I had been working for several years on a collection of B.C. prison writing which, in many ways, centred around the Pen. It was July 15, 1994 and I was going to meet Stephen Duguid, who had been the Director of the SFU Prison Education Programme, and Wayne Knights, who had been one of its coordinators and a lecturer in History. SFU-PEP had been cancelled a year previously and both were now engaged in a research project to evaluate the impact of university education on those prisoners who had been involved with it during its twenty-year history in this province. They had been working in the Archives that morning and were to meet me around noon for lunch at "The Pen": the old Gatehouse had been converted into an up-market coffee house which catered to those who lived in the apartment towers and luxury condominiums that had sprung up on what was formerly the B.C. Pen before its closure in 1980 and I wanted their comments on the manuscript, as well as a guided tour of the site.

I arrived ahead of them and glanced around before I ordered a coffee: on the counter, chained to it, was a copy of *Four Walls in the West,* a history of the penitentiary which had been commissioned by the guards' union; on the walls were various photographs of the B.C. Pen at different points in its history, as well as some aerial photographs which gave an overview of the penitentiary and environs. All that remained now were the gatehouse and the administration building. Everything else had been taken down; only these Gothic fragments, museum pieces, were left behind when the B.C. Pen literally became an invisible city. On the terrace with a coffee, I leafed through the opening pages of an early version of what would become *Sentences and Paroles,* musing over the entries from Warden McBride's diaries as he recorded the operation of his new institution. These mainly humdrum details seemed so at odds with the present situation that it would be easy to imagine that the penitentiary had never existed.

In Xanadu did Kubla Khan
A stately pleasure dome decree:
Where Alph, the sacred river, ran

The ring of new building developments all had postcard views of the Fraser River.

So these five miles of fertile ground
with walls and towers were girdled round:
And there were gardens bright with
sinuous rills.

But what of that other reality which Coleridge saw beneath the surface order and opulence? A "savage place," "with ceaseless turmoil seething," echoing with "Ancestral voices prophesying war" – these phrases would more aptly characterise the turbulent periods in the history of the Penitentiary. Both of these realities somehow co-existed as I moved between *Sentences and Paroles* and the present reality of the B.C. Pen as a "stately pleasure dome."

When Steve and Wayne arrived, we talked about the manuscript for a while and then they took me for an imaginary walkabout of the B.C. Penitentiary. Steve thought that the Royal Engineers cairn had been moved from the front to the rear of the gatehouse and I noticed that its plaque was missing. Steve and Wayne traded notes about where the dome had been situated and reminisced over the countless times they had passed over these spots and the stories they associated with them.

Could I revive within me
Her symphony and song
To such a deep delight 'twould win me,
That with music loud and long,
I would build that dome in air

Steve pointed out a long ravine which ran along the western boundary of the site and where he said you used to be able to hear the guards taking target practice. Coleridge's poem just would not go away – the "Swift half-intermitted burst" which echoed from "that deep romantic chasm which slanted/Down the green hill."

After we finished our tour of the grounds, Steve asked us if we had time to go up to his apartment in one of the towers which overlooked the site. We both had to leave for other appointments and said our goodbyes. I walked back to The Pen Coffee Shop and picked up my briefcase. As I took a farewell glance around, I half-expected to see the gatehouse sign which I had become so accustomed to during the years I had taught at Kent Maximum Security: "Authorized Personnel Only." On the drive home I was reminded of Italo Calvino's meditative comment in *Invisible Cities*: "sometimes different cities follow one another on the same site and under the same name, born and dying without knowing one another, without communication among themselves."

Selected Bibliography

Bruyere, Christian. *Walls*. Vancouver: Talonbooks, 1978.

Calvino, Italo. *Invisible Cities*. Trans. William Weaver. London: Pan Books, 1979.

Chester, Bruce. *Paper Radio: A Book of Poetry*. Penticton: Theytus Books, 1986.

Culhane, Claire. *Barred from Prison*. Vancouver: Pulp Press, 1979.

———. *Still Barred from Prison: Social Injustice in Canada*. Montréal: Black Rose Books, 1985.

———. *No Longer Barred from Prison: Social Injustice in Canada*. A new edition of *Still Barred from Prison*. Montréal: Black Rose Books, 1991.

Davies, Ioan. *Writers in Prison*. Toronto: Between the Lines, 1990.

Dugan, Mark and John Boessenecker. *The Grey Fox: The True Story of Bill Miner – Last of the Old-Time Bandits*. Norman: University of Oklahoma Press, 1992.

Foucault, Michel. *Discipline and Punish: The Birth of the Prison*. Trans. Alan Sheridan. New York: Vintage Books, 1979.

Jackson, Michael. *Prisoners of Isolation: Solitary Confinement in Canada*. Toronto: University of Toronto Press, 1983.

Journal of Prisoners on Prisons 1:1, Summer 1988. Published twice yearly in the summer and winter. It describes its purpose as "to encourage research on a wide range of issues related to crime, justice, and punishment by prisoners and former prisoners."

Murphy, P. J. "Reading and Writing Gaol: The Case of Peter Farrell." *Textual Studies in Canada* I, 1991, pp. 93–107. Reprinted in *Yearbook of Correctional Education, 1992*, pp. 69–82.

Prison Journal, Issues 1–3 (1981–3), published under the aegis of the University of Victoria; Issues 4–10 (1984–1992) published by Institute for the Humanities, Simon Fraser University.

Pollock, Sharon. "One Tiger to a Hill," in *Blood Relations and Other Plays*. Edmonton: NeWest Press, 1981.

Reid, Stephen. *Jackrabbit Parole*. Toronto: Seal Books, 1986.

Richmond, Guy. *Prison Doctor*. Surrey, B.C.: Antonson Publishing, 1975.

Rives, John. *Shackles and Silence: Poems from Prison*. Hamilton, Ontario: Mini Mocho Press, 1992.

Scott, Jack David. *Four Walls In the West: The Story of the British Columbia Penitentiary*. Published as a project of the Retired Prison Officers' Association of British Columbia, 1984.

Serge, Victor. *Men in Prison*. Trans. Richard Greenman. London: Writers and Readers Publishing Cooperative, 1977. First published as *Les hommes dans la prison*, Les Editions Rieter, Paris, 1931.

Schroeder, Andreas. *Shaking It Rough: A Prison Memoir*. Toronto: Doubleday Canada, 1976.

———. *Words Inside Out: Six Poems From a Prison Cycle*. Pamphlet, League of Canadian Poets, 1986.

Transition. Prison magazine "published monthly by the men of the B.C. Penitentiary, New Westminster, B.C." (1952–63). The frontispiece stated: "With the provision that recognition be given *Transition*, permission to reprint anything appearing in this magazine is cordially granted." A set of *Transition* is housed in the University of British Columbia library.

Yates, J. Michael. *The Queen Charlotte Islands Meditations*. Penumbra Press, 1983.

Acknowledgements

"Fall Assizes","The Rossland Courthouse","On the Road, Again","Frame a Day", "Spook","What you are about to hear is True and Faults","looking out a window", "The Man in the Mirror","Wouldn't It Be Fun To Be a Badman?","The Gun", "Make the Body Move","Of the Fittest","Guards Meet the Prisoners","Prison Voltage","My Keeper","The Criminal Code","prison exercise yard (summer)", "Reflections On a Short Career In the Mission Prison Factory","guard tower", "Prison Justice Day, August 10th","The Diver","One, two, three","Noose","Due Process","The Complete Angler","Let It R.I.P.","Time Is a Pecker","The Forgotten Women","Untitled","The Window","Dragon's Teeth","Razor-wire, Millhaven Penitentiary","The Mountains Above Hope","Your Voice","As John Q. Sees Us","Consequences","Poetry In Prison","Telegram From Solitary","The Penthouse","The McWhinney–Ginsburg Correspondence","Inventive Inventories","Dinner At The Keg","On a Photo of Bill","Possibilities","Outfoxed", "Breakfast Near Mission","Polls and Games","Statement of Thomas Mason Shand","The Mediator","To Tom Shand","The Question","Interview With Gerry Hannah","Humanities at Main and Hastings" are reprinted from *Prison Journal* by permission of the respective authors. "Prisoner of Isolation" from Michael Jackson, *Prisoners of Isolation*, reprinted by permission of the author. "Four-Right-Sixteen" from Andreas Schroeder, *Words Inside Out: Six Poems From a Prison Cycle*, reprinted by permission of the author. "Fragments 11 and 19" from Andreas Schroeder, *Shaking It Rough*, reprinted by permission of the author. "day seven" by Dave Emmonds, from *Queen's Quarterly*, Summer 1989, reprinted by permission of the author. "Sentences of Treatment and Sentences of Punishment" from J. Michael Yates, *The Queen Charlotte Islands Meditations*, reprinted by permission of the author. "Industry and Control" from Claire Culhane, *Still Barred From Prison*, reprinted by permission of the author. "The Killing" from Stephen Reid, *Jackrabbit Parole*, reprinted by permission of the author. "The Pen: A Selection of Photographs" by Donald Lawrence, reprinted by permission of the photographer. Archival photographs from the collection of Tony Martin, reprinted by permission. "New Westminster" by Alexander Forbes, reprinted by permission of the author. "Vladimir Ivanovich Meier: Obituary" from Peter N. Maloff, *Dukhobortsy, ikh istoriia, zhizn' i bor'ba (The Doukhobours: Their History, Life and Struggle)*, reprinted by permission of the author. "Walls, Scene 17" from Christian Bruyere, *Walls*, reprinted by permission of the author. "Final Scenes: *One Tiger To a Hill*" from Sharon Pollock, *One Tiger To a Hill*, reprinted by permission of the author. "October 6: The Grand Exit" from Claire Culhane, *Barred From Prison*, reprinted by permission of the author. "From *Still Barred From Prison*" from Claire Culhane, *Still Barred From Prison*, reprinted by permission of the author. "From *No Longer Barred From Prison*" from Claire Culhane, *No Longer Barred From Prison*, reprinted by permission of the author. "A Memorial to Claire" by Tom Elton, from *West Coast Prison Justice Society Newsletter* No. 4, June 1996, reprinted by permission of the author. "Valedictorian Address: B.C. Pen, 1976" by Frank Guiney, from S. Duguid and H. Hoekema, Editors, *University Education in Prison*, reprinted by permission of the author. "Valedictorian Address: Mountain Institution, 1985" by David Turner, from S. Duguid and H. Hoekema, Editors, *University Education in Prison*, reprinted by permission of the author. "Death on the Installment Plan" and "Valuable Program Cut" by Wayne Knights, reprinted by permission of the author. "Killing prison's SFU program a giant leap backwards" by Bob MacDonald, reprinted by permission of the author. "The Cranes" and "RUSS II" by Vladimir Meier, from *Moskva* (Chicago, IL), Vol. 1, No. 10, 1929, and Vol. 2, No. 3, 1930, reprinted by permission of the author's estate. (170–171)